THE 4MM COAL WAGON

A STEP-BY-STEP GUIDE

BY

JOHN HAYES

WILD SWAN PUBLICATIONS LTD.

CONTENTS

© Wild Swan Publications Ltd. and John Hayes 1999
ISBN: 1 874103 48 8

Designed by Paul Karau
Printed by Amadeus Press, Huddersfield

Published by
WILD SWAN PUBLICATIONS LIMITED
1-3 Hagbourne Road, Didcot, Oxon, OX11 8DP

This picture of improvement work at Bathampton on 21st September 1942, and the picture overleaf taken at Leamington on 9th January 1948, are both enlarged areas of broader scenes, and feature an entirely random selection of private owner coal wagons after the wartime pooling. With all the different wagon builders, varying designs of successive generations and the multitude of liveries, the essence of any train of private owner wagons was variety. Even fleets of nominally similar vehicles in a common livery seem to have no end of differences. The 8-plank Denaby wagon in the picture above looks similar to the portrait on the left, but there are all sorts of detail differences.
NATIONAL
RAILWAY MUSEUM

Two more modern 8-plank wagons from the Denaby fleet and again more differences to study. These pictures and the one opposite were all taken in the 1950s and show varying degrees of the original pre-war livery of red oxide with white lettering shaded black. They had all been fitted with various replacement planks and whereas the one on the opposite page and the one on the left show successive styles of P series numbering, the one above had survived apparently without even having received the wartime pool lettering. These variations provide wonderful subjects for modelling.

ROYE ENGLAND and J. A. G. H. COLTAS

More privately owned coal wagons, this time in a down goods train hauled by a Metropolitan Railway 'K' class 2–6–4T and passing Deep Mill bridge, Great Missenden, c.1938.

S. H. FREESE

INTRODUCTION

This book began as a *Model Railway Journal* commissioned article intended to show how to improve a few private owner wagon kits. Up to this time, most of my modelling activity had been involved with building layouts for exhibition and making models for other people. This commission seemed like an opportunity to actually build something for myself using up some of the stock of wagon kits which I had tucked away for my eventual layout.

I had only built the odd one or two wagons, and my knowledge of the subject was rather scanty, so I began by swotting-up, using most of the published material and soon began to realise that building two or three wagons would only scratch the surface. Also, with the development in recent years of add-on bits and pieces, i.e. etched brake gear and suspension systems, it was obvious that it would be impossible to cover all these variations and developments in one article. It was therefore suggested that I carried on with the project which would be produced as a small book instead.

Why only coal wagons?, one may ask. Well, up to the 1960s, coal was the predominant mineral traffic on the railways of Britain, so anyone modelling the traditional steam railway, will need a fair percentage of coal wagons as part of their freight stock. Gas works and power stations used vast amounts of coal whilst it was also the main fuel for domestic heating, and nearly all supplies were transported by rail. As an example, my own chosen prototype, the small branch terminus at Wallingford, received an average of 10-12 wagon loads of coal per day. So I would need a minimum of 24 wagons, and more if I am to ring the changes and make operation more interesting. Therefore, thirty or more mineral wagons would not be out of place.

There are plenty of pre-printed kits and transfers for numerous collieries and traders, but it is difficult to find which ones are appropriate to your chosen period and for how long these wagons carried a particular livery. For instance, there doesn't seem much point in building a Vauxhall Colliery wagon for a late 1930s layout when the colliery closed in 1928 and the wagons were presumably sold off and repainted.

Official works photographs, i.e. the Gloucester and Charles Roberts collections, are fine up to a point, but it is

Left: *Two of the scratch-built models made for this book by methods described later.* Below: *Two early prototype wagons from the extensive Eckington fleet. These were painted red oxide with white lettering shaded black, but careful study of pictures confirms that in later years some Eckington wagons had plain white lettering as portrayed in both models.*

far from clear how long the various liveries survived. The only reliable source is careful study of period photographs in which wagons often appear in the background.

Broadly speaking, up to the outbreak of the Second World War, private owner wagons carried their owners' chosen and sometimes elaborate livery. After 1939, the PO wagon fleet was pooled and became common user, the condition of the wagons gradually deteriorating. In order to preserve their identity, the owners' names were painted in small white lettering at the bottom left-hand corner of the wagon sides, the intention being to return the wagons to their original owners after the war had finished. In the event, this was not to be, and when the railways were nationalised in 1948, the PO wagons became the property of British Railways and were given new numbers with 'P' prefixes.

From a modelling point of view, this can be a fascinating period, as wagons of many different liveries can be run together. In the early BR years, many wagons could be observed carrying remains of their original livery with wartime lettering and also the BR 'P' numbers. No repainting was undertaken at this time, only patch repairs to keep them serviceable. From the middle to late 1950s, they were dwindling rapidly and standard steel minerals were built to replace them. Obviously, this is only the most sweeping overview and I refer the reader to the bibliography at the end of this book for a fuller picture on this subject. In fact, the publications listed are my main source of information.

I have tried to describe the various aspects of wagon construction from simple kit modification to full scratch-

building, using many of the available after-market bits and pieces available today. Also, with the aid of simple jigs and fixtures, I hope I have shown how time and effort can be saved.

Whilst this book deals with coal wagons, the methods are equally applicable to other types of wagon in any scale or gauge.

In order to illustrate this book, I have built about thirty models ranging from early wooden types to a few examples of steel minerals. I have attempted to illustrate the constructional methods using step-by-step photographs which I hope will prove more helpful than words alone, but the reader must be the final judge.

I have tried to show as many methods as possible, to the extent that some of the ideas described I may not use again. However, I felt it best to show everything as I progressed and let readers pick out the bits they prefer.

Finally, I must thank my good friend Brian Clark for reading through much of my scribbled text and for offering helpful advice, also Paul and June at Wild Swan for their kindness and hospitality; without Paul's gentle persuasion and encouragement over the last couple of years, I doubt whether I would have considered writing anything. I still don't find it easy and prefer making things to writing about them. I hope this volume will prove useful and interesting and that it might perhaps encourage modellers to build and improve their own wagons.

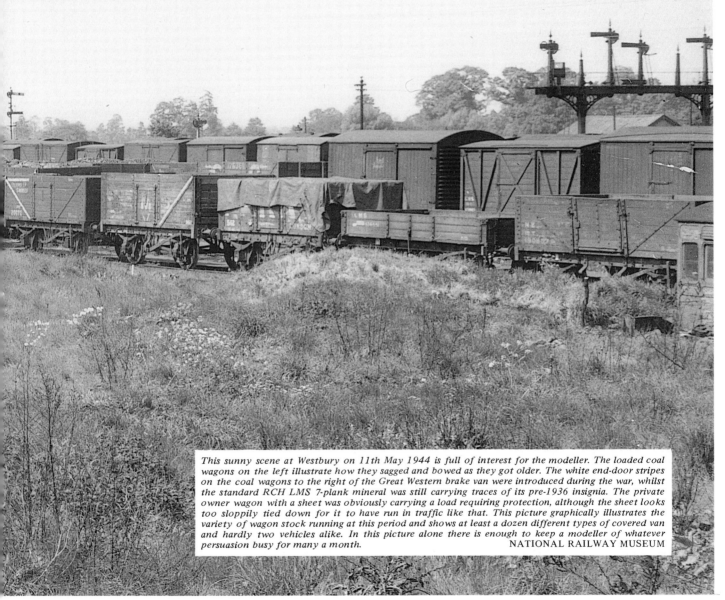

This sunny scene at Westbury on 11th May 1944 is full of interest for the modeller. The loaded coal wagons on the left illustrate how they sagged and bowed as they got older. The white end-door stripes on the coal wagons to the right of the Great Western brake van were introduced during the war, whilst the standard RCH LMS 7-plank mineral was still carrying traces of its pre-1936 insignia. The private owner wagon with a sheet was obviously carrying a load requiring protection, although the sheet looks too sloppily tied down for it to have run in traffic like that. This picture graphically illustrates the variety of wagon stock running at this period and shows at least a dozen different types of covered van and hardly two vehicles alike. In this picture alone there is enough to keep a modeller of whatever persuasion busy for many a month.
NATIONAL RAILWAY MUSEUM

The portable work area in use on the dining room table.

TOOLS AND MATERIALS

Only simple tools are needed for this sort of modelling and everyone will have their own preferences. I will only list the basic tools I use, whilst the home-made jigs and fixtures which I have found useful are described in the course of the text.

The most essential consideration is a comfortable well-lit work area. If you have a permanent bench, that's fine, but a portable work table which can be set up anywhere can easily be made from a sheet of ¾in MDF board, about 2ft square, with some timber edging on three sides to contain everything. Most of the models described in this book were made using just such a board. Good light is essential and I now use a pair of Anglepoise lamps fitted with 15 watt low energy bulbs. These give excellent light and stay cool, unlike ordinary bulbs which can be uncomfortable, especially while doing close work.

A good quality cutting mat is a real boon when working with styrene sheet and plastic kits. It is much better than using a scrap of hardboard or card which soon gets into a mess. Mine is A3 and covers any size I am likely to cut; smaller sizes are available. It is made by Edding, and whilst there are cheaper mats on the market, I find them too soft and they do not last as well.

I always use Swann-Morton scalpels in preference to normal modelling knives which I find cumbersome. However, this is only my opinion; in the end, use whatever is most comfortable. For general cutting, I use 10A and 15A blades, and a No. 10 for removing detail and as a scraper. Used in the standard No. 3 handle, they are excellent to work with. A retractable handle is also available, which is safer when not in use and protects the blade. I always buy blades in boxes of 100 as they are much cheaper this way.

I always use Slater's styrene with Mek-pak solvent and have found these products totally reliable. There are alternatives available but some of the sheet materials are of variable quality. I prefer to stick with a dependable product.

Slater's produce a range of micro-strip but for the models described in this book I have used materials from the Evergreen range, which includes strip, sections, scribed sheet, etc. They are also the only

suppliers of 0.005in sheet that I know of today. When using Mek-pak, I decant a small amount into a little glass pill bottle which sits in a simple stand made from 0.060in styrene. This is virtually impossible to knock over on the workbench, unlike the standard bottle.

An engineers square is necessary and I use 3in and 6in sizes, the small one for most jobs and the larger one for cutting sheet materials, etc. A 6in stainless steel rule is also required; this is better than ordinary steel which soon becomes tarnished and difficult to read. A 12in

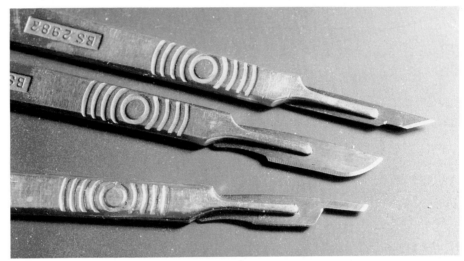

Swann-Morton scalpels. From the top, a 15A blade for general cutting, a No. 10 for scraping, and at the bottom a modified No. 10 blade ideal for removing plastic detail.

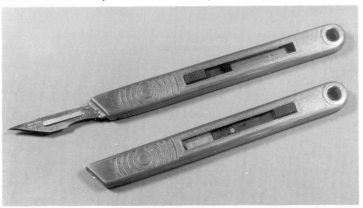

The retractable scalpel.

Mek-pak dispenser.

rule is also useful for long cutting jobs on sheet materials and as a straight edge when scribing styrene, etc.

In my view, a vernier caliper is an indispensable tool for modelmaking and, if you really want to push the boat out, a micrometer. The vernier is probably better if only one precision measuring tool is required as it can measure inside, outside and depth plus a larger size range from 0in—6in upwards, depending on the size. A dial version is probably easier to use as measurements are read direct from a dial instead of having to work them out from a vernier scale, which can be a bit of a mystery until you get the hang of it. An inexpensive one will be perfectly accurate enough for our sort of work.

I personally like to use a micrometer for measuring diameters such as drill shanks, wire thicknesses, etc. I feel they are more accurate than a vernier because of the wider measuring faces. However, micrometers have a small range, 1in or 25mm, irrespective of their size, and are only able to measure outside diameters, so the vernier is probably quite adequate for most modellers.

A pair of 6in engineer's dividers are very useful for marking out and transferring measurements, etc.

A few good quality files are essential. Buy the best you can afford as they will repay the cost many times over. This applies to any tools. I use Swiss-made files from Vallorbe and Oberg, which are available from Shestos. A fairly coarse flat file will quickly remove detail such as moulded W-irons and underfloor detail from plastic kits.

A small selection of flat, half-round and round needle files in No. 2 and No. 4 cuts are ideal.

As well as files, I have a selection of home-made emery boards for general sanding, and smoothing plastic and metal parts. These are simply made from thin plastic sheet or 2-3mm thick wood cut into strips about 6in long and ½in wide. Various grades of silicon carbide paper are stuck to these with double-sided adhesive tape.

A selection of small drills from 0.5mm to 2mm are essential and I also have several pin chucks to use them in, which saves having to keep changing drills. Pin chucks are also useful for holding wire, etc, when working on it. Most of the drilling is done by hand and I only use a powered mini-drill with burrs or cutting discs.

A small smooth-jawed vice is very helpful for holding and bending etched components, as are smooth-jawed pliers.

Some good stout-bladed tweezers are useful; try to avoid fine-pointed ones which are not much use.

For cutting sheet metal, I prefer to use a piercing saw in preference to snips, which distort the metal and, in my view, can do more harm than good. A scrawker ground up from a piece of hacksaw blade is an excellent tool for cutting straight lines in thin sheet. For general cutting of wire, etches, etc, the Xuron micro-shears are superb.

Apart from Mek-pak solvent, I use Devcon 5-minute epoxy adhesive for quick one-off jobs. This cures very quickly, so when fitting several parts, I now use a 1-hour epoxy which has a working time of about 20 minutes. This is available from good general model shops dealing with aircraft and boat modelling. I also use superglue and have found Zap-a-gap, available from Fourtrack Models, the best to date. However, I only use superglue on small details.

The soldering iron I have used for many years is a Weller industrial iron; the current model is TCP/PS.3D. These are only available through the electronic suppliers such as Maplins. I have used these irons for all model work from delicate parts like etched brakegear to 7mm locomotive building and would recommend them to anyone. A wide range of tip shapes and temperatures is available; the one I use most is a No. 7, 2.5mm spade (Weller PT.BB).

I have used Carr's 145° solder and Green Label flux for all general soldering described here and have found these products totally satisfactory.

Two home-made tools from old hacksaw blades. Top: *A scrawker for cutting thin sheet metal.* Below: *A tool for cutting etched parts from frets. Used on an offcut of hard plastic laminate such as Formica, this will cut parts out cleanly and without risk of distortion.*

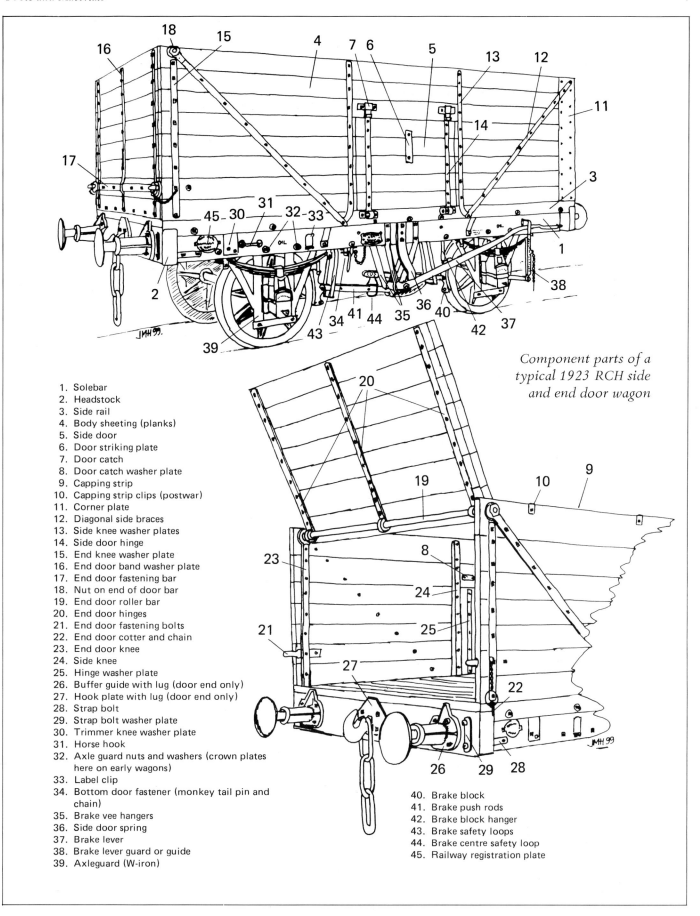

Component parts of a typical 1923 RCH side and end door wagon

1. Solebar
2. Headstock
3. Side rail
4. Body sheeting (planks)
5. Side door
6. Door striking plate
7. Door catch
8. Door catch washer plate
9. Capping strip
10. Capping strip clips (postwar)
11. Corner plate
12. Diagonal side braces
13. Side knee washer plates
14. Side door hinge
15. End knee washer plate
16. End door band washer plate
17. End door fastening bar
18. Nut on end of door bar
19. End door roller bar
20. End door hinges
21. End door fastening bolts
22. End door cotter and chain
23. End door knee
24. Side knee
25. Hinge washer plate
26. Buffer guide with lug (door end only)
27. Hook plate with lug (door end only)
28. Strap bolt
29. Strap bolt washer plate
30. Trimmer knee washer plate
31. Horse hook
32. Axle guard nuts and washers (crown plates here on early wagons)
33. Label clip
34. Bottom door fastener (monkey tail pin and chain)
35. Brake vee hangers
36. Side door spring
37. Brake lever
38. Brake lever guard or guide
39. Axleguard (W-iron)
40. Brake block
41. Brake push rods
42. Brake block hanger
43. Brake safety loops
44. Brake centre safety loop
45. Railway registration plate

Finding a photograph of a wagon which matches the kit you have and that is also suitable for your chosen period is not always easy. This J. R. Wood wagon, photographed at Cardington on 11th October 1939, could be modelled using the Slater's kit for a Charles Roberts 7-plank end-door wagon. The livery was noted as orange with black lettering.

WESSEX COLLECTION

KIT-BUILT WAGONS

At the time of writing, plastic kits are available for private owner mineral wagons from Cambrian and Slaters. These include the 1923 RCH standard 7-plank wagons and a range of earlier types from Charles Roberts and the Gloucester Carriage and Wagon Co. in 5, 6 and 7-plank versions. Both manufacturers offer a small range of pre-printed kits with colliery and traders' names.

In whitemetal, ABS offer the RCH 1923 wagons in both 7 and 8-plank versions plus the LNER and LMS standard minerals which were built to the 1923 design. Parkside Dundas also produce a range of steel-bodied mineral wagons. I shall describe these wagons here, but there are many company-owned mineral wagons and opens available from other manufacturers, and the techniques described can be used for many types.

SLATER'S

Slater's kits are very finely moulded but they have no internal detail except the floors. If the wagons are to be modelled loaded, this is not a problem, but, if left empty, they look rather plain inside.

It is easier to apply this detail before assembling the body. If the wagon has pre-printed lettering, I give it a protective coat of matt varnish, either Humbrol or Ronseal matt coat thinned with pure turpentine. Some of the wagons were lettered with POWsides rub-down transfers, which I applied before assembling the wagon as per instructions. However, I have found it just as easy to apply these after assembly and painting

of the model, hence there is less chance of damage to the lettering.

Before assembly, the first thing to do is scribe the internal plank detail. I use a pair of dividers to transfer the positions of the outside planks to the inside. The points of the dividers need to be quite

Slater's Gloucester 5-plank wagon with POWsides lettering. Measuring the position of the outside planks with dividers.

sharp to scribe the lines all along the sides and ends. These are then deepened slightly with a scoring tool. Mine is made from a piece of power hacksaw blade. Light strokes are taken until the required depth of line is achieved. When all the lines were scribed, I gave the side a gentle rub-over

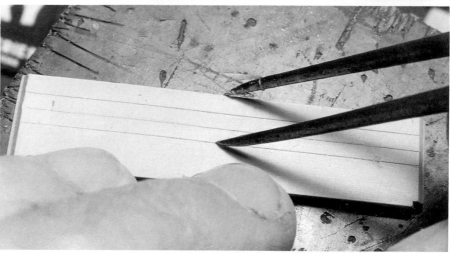

Transferring the measurements to the inside.

Here is the tool used for scoring plank lines.

with a fine emery stick to remove any burrs, followed by a rub with a fibreglass brush to finish off.

I scribed the vertical lines to show the side door in the same way, then fitted the internal ironwork, although in future I would do this after assembly of the body, as I did for the scratchbuilt models described later. Most of the internal ironwork is cut from 0.005in x 0.030in styrene, which I cut using a simple jig as described in the scratchbuilding chapter.

Internal ironwork does vary considerably and can only be deduced from pictures. Unfortunately, they are not too common, so a bit of guesstimation is sometimes the order of the day.

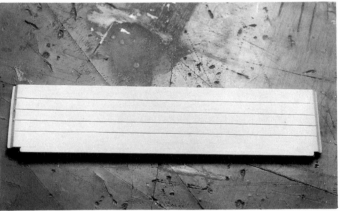

Left: This shows the tool in use following the lines marked with dividers. Right: Gloucester 5-plank wagon. The scored plank lines have been cleaned up.

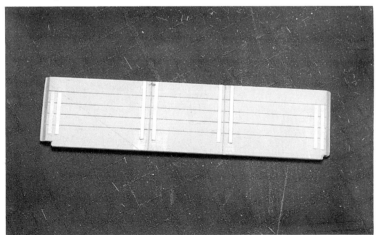

The vertical door lines have been scribed and the vertical ironwork fitted, leaving clearance for the floor. I now do this after assembly of the body.

Drilling the hole for the end door bar.

These two pictures show the side and end of a 1923 RCH 7-plank wagon ready for assembly. A 0.6mm hole has been drilled for the end door bar.

A 1942 line-up of mineral wagons, showing some internal details. The wagon at the bottom provides an example of narrow corner plates, whilst the next two had been fitted with the more common wide type. The next mineral wagon had been converted for merchandise traffic. During the Second World War, due to a shortage of merchandise wagons, the LMS and LNER converted a number of wagons by removing the top planks above the side door to aid loading. The side door was increased in height by one plank. Note also the 'T' section end stanchions. A number of PO wagons were also converted in a similar way.

NATIONAL
RAILWAY MUSEUM

Using side cutters to remove the bulk of the underframe detail.

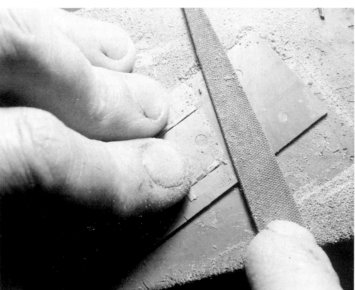

The rest is removed with a coarse file.

Before assembling the body, I remove all the moulded underframe detail from the floor, unless, of course, the model is to be built with a rigid underframe. As all the wagons described in this book are fitted with compensation or sprung suspension, a flat floor is necessary. If the wagon is to be loaded, a plain floor cut from 0.040in styrene would do the job.

The bulk of the detail is cut away with side cutters (I use Xuron micro shears). This looks a bit brutal but it gets most of it off quickly, and then I finish off with a coarse flat file.

I use an emery stick to clean up the mitred corners and ensure a good fit before assembling the body around the floor.

The rest of the internal ironwork is fitted, i.e. diagonals and internal top corner plates, then I give the top edges of the wagon sides a smooth-off with an

Here is the body assembled with internal ironwork finished and capping strips fitted.

emery stick and fit capping strips of 0.005in x 0.030in strip, which finish off the top and cover over the corner joints.

The buffer mouldings on these kits are quite acceptable and can be used as supplied if you just want rigid buffers. I like to spring mine, and this is quite easy.

I first smooth the ends of the buffer stocks with a fine emery board or file, in order to give a flat face for the plastic collars which are supplied as separate items in the kit.

The stocks were drilled 1mm dia to take MJT buffer heads. Before fitting the

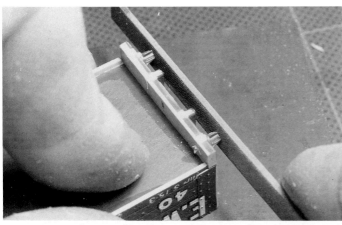 

Left: *Smoothing off the ends of the buffer stocks with a fine emery stick.* Right: *Drilling the buffer stocks 1mm diameter.*

Left: *Gloucester 5-plank wagon. This shows the short lengths of 1mm brass wire fitted to locate the end collars.* Right: *When the collars have hardened off, they are smoothed off with fine silicon carbide paper. The ends can be lightly countersunk. This is a 1923 RCH 7-plank wagon with POWsides lettering. The solebars/axleboxes have been modified for sprung suspension. This will be described later.*

collars I pushed in short lengths of 1mm dia brass wire into the stocks, then slid on the collars and fixed them with solvent. This ensures they will be true with the hole and it is easier than just sticking them on. I let these harden thoroughly before removing the brass wires; the plastic will not stick to the brass. The collars are then smoothed off with a fold of fine silicon carbide paper.

At this stage, the solebars can be fitted, but a decision must be made as to which type of suspension system is to be used, because this will determine the spacing of the solebars. Most etched W-irons and Exactoscale springing units are 24mm wide but the Masokits units are 25mm wide. It is also important to decide on the type of axlebox springs required. For the wagons described here, I have retained the moulded axlebox and spring and only removed the moulded W-iron. This is described in detail in the chapter on underframes (see page 68).

This 1923 RCH wagon clearly shows the buffer and coupling plate extensions at the door end to protect the end floor boards when tipping. Note the odd axleboxes. A. ATTEWELL

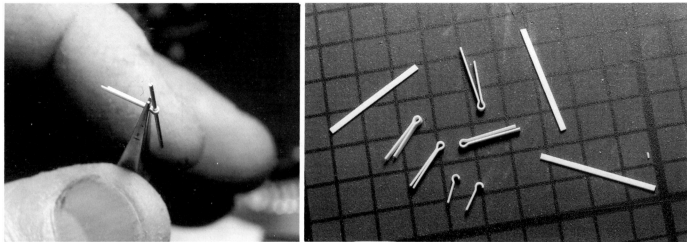

Left: *Hinge bar clips gripped around 0.7mm wire with tweezers.* Right: *This is the result after immersion in near-boiling water. The pieces at the bottom are the parts cut from them for the tops of the hinges.*

Right: *A 1923 RCH 7-plank wagon with door hinge bar fitted and nuts at each end. Far right: RCH 1923 7-plank wagon sides and ends assembled and top edge cleaned up.*

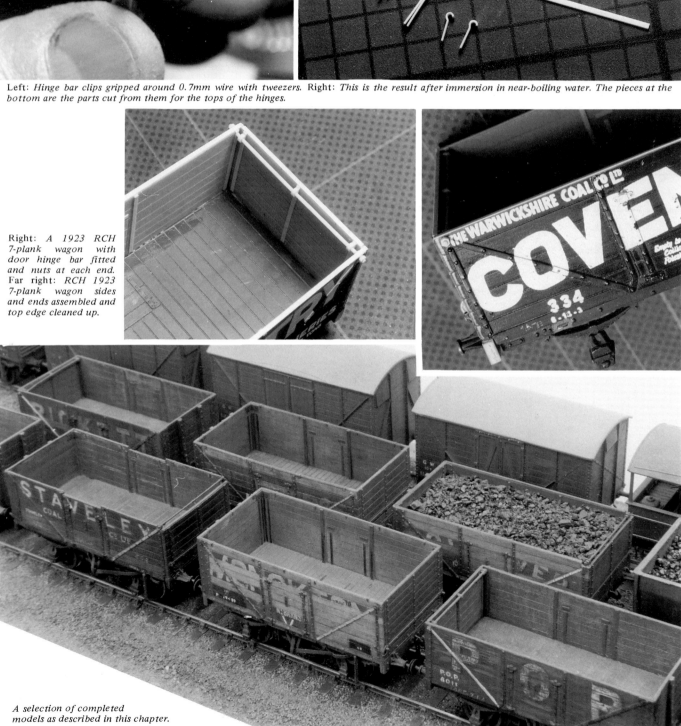

A selection of completed models as described in this chapter.

Two POP wagons, both lettered with POWsides transfers. The wagon on the left has the wartime insignia, i.e. the name repeated in small letters at the left-hand side. The right-hand wagon has the top plank modified to the 'London' type.

Left: *A completed model from a Slater's RCH 7-plank with POWsides lettering.*

The end door hinge bars as supplied look a bit heavy, so I replaced them with home-made components. The top sections of the vertical door bands, which on the real wagons wrap round the hinge bar, are made from 0.010in x 0.030in strip (Evergreen 101). I cut a supply of pieces about 15mm long and fold them around a short length of 0.7mm brass wire and grip them with tweezers. They are then held in near-boiling water for a second and cooled in cold water.

I fill the kettle and bring it to the boil, switch off, and, with the lid removed, dunk in the parts to be formed. I find this an excellent way to produce these sorts of bits and pieces. Needless to say, take great care when doing this.

The hinge bar is made from 0.025in rod (Evergreen 219) which was made overlong, and a nut cut from 0.020in styrene was fitted at each end.

The underframe details are described in a separate chapter.

A Sully & Co. wagon starting to lose its identity with unpainted replacement planks. Note also the gap filler below the door.

A side-door-only wagon.

A typical coal train at King's Cross York Road in April 1939. Note the Rickett wagon has the 'S' omitted. R. F. ROBERTS

Two more Ricketts wagons. Note the lowered top plank above the side door, known as the London plank. The wagon above was built by Chas Roberts & Co. Note the differences in the vertical ironwork at the side of the door on these two wagons.

COLLECTION
R. S. CARPENTER

LENS OF SUTTON

CAMBRIAN

To illustrate the Cambrian kits, I have built a couple of 1923 RCH side and end-door wagons and a Gloucester 7-plank side-door type. They are all pre-printed, the RCH versions from Cambrian's own range, and the Gloucester wagon is one of a range produced by Cambrian exclusively for R. D. Whyborn Models of Redditch.

As with all the wagons described here, I built the bodies, including the solebars and headstocks, and fitted the running gear afterwards (see page 55). As with the Slater's kits, the lettering was given a protective coat of varnish before starting.

The mouldings are very good and only require a little fettling to ensure a good fit at the corners. I try to get the corner plates fitting tightly as these will be rounded-off slightly when the solvent has dried thoroughly. The sides and ends were assembled without the floor this time as this did not quite fit. I use a small amount of solvent on the corner joints initially, just to hold them together. They may need tweaking a little to get everything square. It is better to ensure that the corner plates and planks line up even if the top edges don't quite match.

When all is well, a brushful of solvent down each joint finishes them off and I put the body aside to harden. The top edges of the body are smoothed off with an emery stick and the corner plates rounded off slightly.

The sides on these kits are a bit over-scale in thickness, so I chamfered the inside top edges slightly to disguise this. Capping strips are fitted later to cover the top edges.

The floors are used as supplied and it was only necessary to remove the moulding pips underneath. However, as I said before, the floors did not fit too well and needed adjusting, either by removing some material or adding some to fill a gap.

I decided to replace the headstocks on these wagons and made new ones from

A model of a typical Ricketts wagon from a pre-printed Cambrian kit.

The floor fitted. Note the packing strips at the bottom and right.

 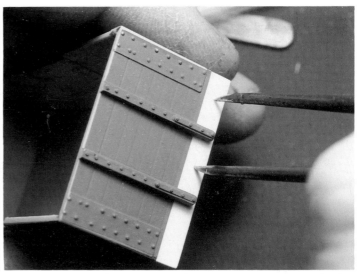

Left: *Here the corner plates have been rounded slightly and the new headstock fitted. A 0.5mm diameter hole in the centre marks the hook position.* Right: *Buffer positions are marked from the hook position with dividers.*

 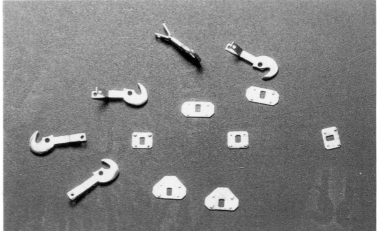

Left: *Ambis coupling plates.* Right: *Hooks and plates ready for fitting.*

Left: *A hook and plate fitted. The plate is secured with a spot of superglue.* Right: *The tails of the hook are bent over and will be secured with epoxy when the buffers are fitted.*

Left: *This is a Gloucester side-door wagon from R. D. Whyborn Models based on the Cambrian kit.*

Below: *These wagons had threaded extensions to the internal diagonals which protruded through the ends. I drilled these out 0.6mm and fitted stubs of 0.025in styrene rod.*

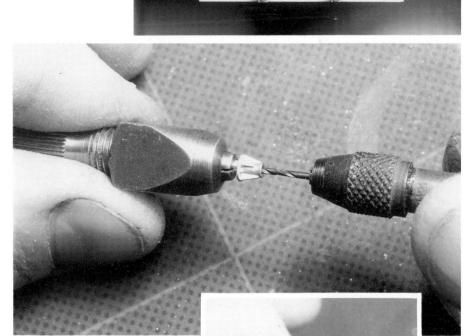

Drilling buffer stocks 1mm diameter.

This shows the result.

0.060in x 0.156in styrene (Evergreen 157). The ones in the kits were not very good mouldings, and the buffers would need replacing anyway as the moulded ones looked a bit scrawny.

When the headstocks were fitted, I used a pair of dividers to mark the centre and drilled a 0.5mm hole. From this I marked the buffer centres 23mm apart and drilled these 0.5mm. These were opened out to suit the buffers and hooks.

I use coupling hooks and plates from Ambis Engineering. Masokits and MJT Components also supply etched coupling hooks. Cast ones are available from ABS. I find it easier to drill a hole large enough to take the shank of the hook in the headstock rather than mess about cutting slots. The hook plate locates the hook, and, with the ends of the drawbar bent over inside and secured with a dob of epoxy, the job is easy.

Buffers used on these kits are from the ABS range — FU12 for the 1923 RCH wagons and FU13 for the Gloucester wagons. These are not difficult to convert to springing. I first cut off the heads, then file the end of the stock flat. The shank of the housing is then held in a pin chuck and, using a second pin chuck, drilled 1mm dia right through, taking care to keep the drill straight and in the centre of the body. I countersink the end slightly just for appearance sake, using a larger drill, about 2mm dia.

The buffer housings were fitted next. I drilled the holes in the headstocks slightly undersize, then opened them out with a round file until the housing was a fairly tight fit. Before gluing them in place, I shortened the shanks so they did

ABS early PO buffers (FU13) fitted to a Gloucester 7-plank wagon.

not protrude through the back of the headstocks. I use 1-hour epoxy to secure them as the 5-minute variety goes off too fast for my liking.

I make buffer spring retainers from 0.020in styrene strip about 2mm wide, cut into pieces approx 6mm long, with a 0.5mm hole drilled close to one end (see photos).

These are fixed to the back of the headstock with a buffer head in place to line up the hole. They can be adjusted as necessary to ensure the buffer shanks are both square with the headstock and truly horizontal.

The buffer heads and springs are not fitted until the wagon is finished. The heads and springs are from MJT Components' 13in heads (2371) for RCH 1923 wagons, and 12in heads (2370) for earlier vehicles. The springs may need tweaking a little, either stretching slightly or shortening to get as soft an action as possible.

Back now to body details. The end-door bars on these wagons are a different type to the Slater's RCH 1923 pattern. This time the ends of the top plank are cut away and the hinge bar retained by

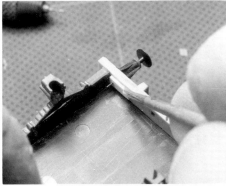

Left: *A supply of buffer spring retainers.* Right: *Fitting the retainers to the wagon using a buffer head (MJT) for location.*

This jumps ahead and shows how the heads are finally retained with a slice of plastic sleeving cut from electrical wire. I prefer this to bending the shank over. It is easier to set the length of buffers and makes replacement easy should they get damaged. The sleeve can be secured with a tiny spot of cyano.

Cambrian 1923 RCH wagon showing the type of end-door hinge bar compared to the Slater's type. The moulded bar has yet to be removed.

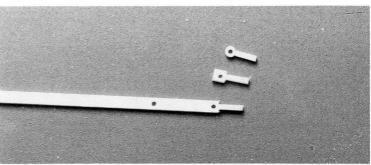

Stages in making the end knee extensions.

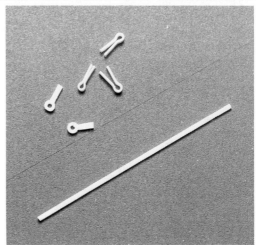

This shows the components of a hinge bar, end knee extensions, door bar and door band clips.

A standard 1923 RCH 7-plank wagon at Cardington on 23rd October 1939. The livery was red oxide with white lettering shaded black.

This shows the parts assembled on the wagon. This is not totally accurate but looks much better than the original.

Left: *Bar retaining clips made up from pieces of 0.010in styrene.* Right: *After cleaning up.*

The inside of P370033, a similar wagon to that described here. Note the diagonal extensions to the end knees and the capping strip retaining clips.

A Rickett wagon built from the Slater's kit, lettered with POWsides transfers, and on the right the Cambrian pre-printed version.

joggled clips bolted to the sides. On the real wagons, the tops of the end knees inside the body had a forged eye to support the bar. These are represented on the model by pieces cut from 0.015in styrene. I drilled a series of 0.6mm holes along a strip, then cut out the pieces as shown on page 21.

The three clips along the bar, which represent the tops of the vertical door band, were made in the same way as for the Slater's kit.

The end-door bar-retaining clips are made from scraps of 0.010in x 0.030in strip which were trimmed up after they had hardened off.

I used the solebars from the kit, only removing the moulded outside V-hangers which I replaced with etched components, as described later (page 78).

Another Cambrian pre-lettered wagon.

A Gloucester 7-plank side-door wagon from a limited edition from R. D. Whyborn based on the Cambrian kit.

This wagon, at first glance, looks like a standard RCH LNER mineral. It was in fact an ex-Great Central Railway 6-plank. Note the arrangement of planking and the end door retaining bar which pivoted at its centre and latched at the end. There was still a vestige of the large diagonal stripe and large letters 'NE'.

LNER/LMS MINERALS

The Cambrian kit of the 1923 RCH wagon makes a good basis for models of the LNER and LMS standard mineral wagons. Many thousands of these were built during the 1920s and '30s to the RCH 1923 specification. They had iron T-section end stanchions instead of wood; some PO wagons were also fitted with iron stanchions. The LNER vehicles were not fitted with bottom doors, so the floor from the kit will need replacing if the wagon is modelled empty.

Construction of the body is the same as the Cambrian PO wagons, but this time I have improved the end-door retaining bar as the fit of the kit in this area is not very good.

Before assembly, the recesses in the ends of the sides were filled in with a scrap of styrene. When this had hardened, I filed it smooth and reinstated the plank grooves with a scalpel. The ends of the bar on the door were also removed and replacements fitted after assembly of the body.

The bulk of the wooden stanchion mouldings on the fixed end were cut away with side cutters and the rest removed with a fine file. I reinstated the plank grooves with the tool shown on page 10.

The bodies were assembled as for the previous Cambrian kits, but to avoid the bottom doors, the LNER version had a new floor cut from scribed styrene, 0.040in x 0.080in spacing (Evergreen 4080).

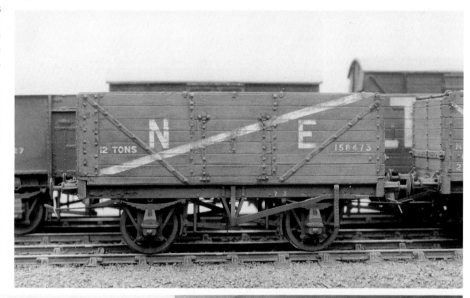

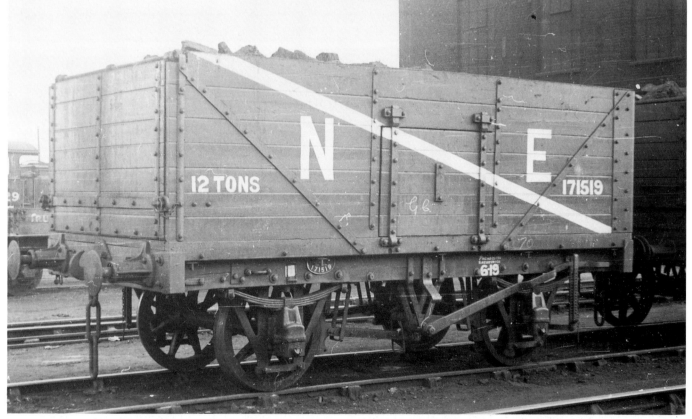

Here are a model and the real thing in the pre-1936 LNER livery, i.e. large 'NE' and white diagonal stripe to identify the end door. This always sloped up to the top of the end door.
COLLECTION R. J. ESSERY

Left: *Gaps in the ends of the sides filled with a scrap of styrene.* Middle: *This is cleaned up and the plank grooves cut in.* Right: *End door on the left with bar ends removed.*

Removing most of the end stanchions.

Right: *The end after cleaning-up and plank grooves scored. The body has been assembled and new headstock fitted.* Far right: *The door end of the same wagon.*

Left: This is the LMS version with bottom doors using the original floor. *Right:* Here is the LNER one with a replacement floor from scribed styrene. I have also thinned down the top edges of the sides which improves their appearance.

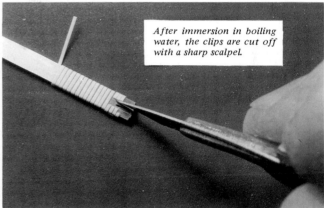

Strip wound round a piece of 1mm x 3mm brass.

After immersion in boiling water, the clips are cut off with a sharp scalpel.

Headstocks were once again Evergreen and followed the same procedure as the previous Cambrian kits. I used some surplus Slater's 1923 RCH underframe kits for the solebars, axleboxes and springs for these wagons (see the chapter on underframes).

Capping strip from 0.005in x 0.030in strips were fitted as before, but this time I decided to add the retaining clips which were a feature from about the national-isation period. These clips are easily made using 0.005in x 0.020in styrene strip wound tightly around a short piece of 1mm x 3mm brass strip. A saw cut in the end of the brass holds the strip while it is wound round, then held tight with tweezers and immersed in boiling water for a couple of seconds and cooled under a cold tap.

The clips were cut off with a sharp scalpel and fitted to the top of the wagon with a touch of solvent.

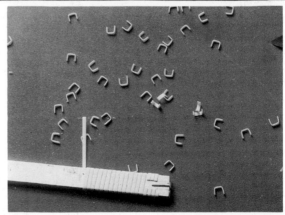

This is the result.

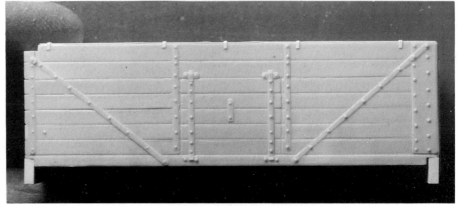

Here are the clips fitted to the model.

The new end stanchions were made up from 0.010in x 0.060in (Evergreen 103) for the vertical centre strip, and two strips of 0.010in x 0.030in (Evergreen 101) for the flanges each side.

Bolt head detail on the end stanchions was represented by slicing some impressed rivets from a piece of 0.010in sheet and fixing them to the model with solvent; an alternative would be to cut some 'dots' from a sliver of 0.010in styrene and use these instead.

Here is a model of a wagon in bauxite livery with the post-1936 lettering and small white stripe to indicate the end door. The lettering and bottom door markings are Methfix transfers.

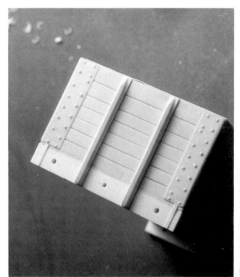

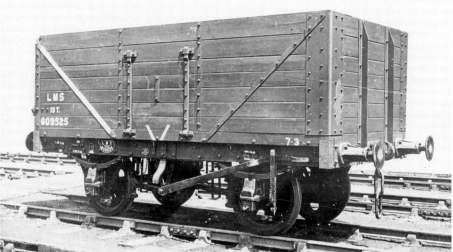

New end stanchions fitted and washer plates at the ends of the headstocks, and the real thing which clearly shows the 'T' end stanchions.
COLLECTION R. J. ESSERY

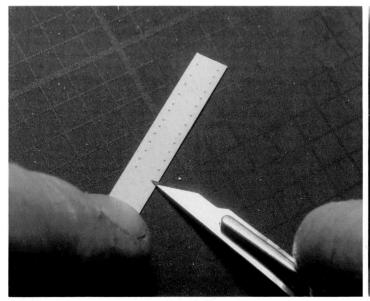

Left: *Slicing rivets from a piece of 0.010in sheet.* Right: *This shows the rivets fixed to the end stanchions.*

This is how these wagons first appeared in service, grey livery, large 'LMS' and no white stripe, c.1924.
COLLECTION
R. J. ESSERY

A model of a wagon similar to that above, but with the addition of the white stripe. These large stripes were made by painting some clear transfer film with white acrylic ink and cutting strips from them. Note also the battered capping strip and clips.

Here is a wagon in grey livery with small 'LMS' and large stripe, photographed in 1939. Note also the grab handles on the end door, a feature of LMS mineral wagons.
COLLECTION
R. J. ESSERY

Punch for door bar ends.

This photo clearly shows the end door hinge bar retainer on these wagons.
COLLECTION
R. J. ESSERY

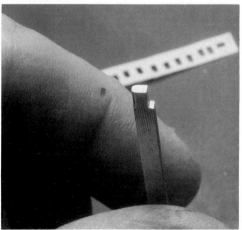

The ends of the end-door bars were replaced with little punchings from 0.010in sheet. The punch is filed from a piece of mild steel and used on an offcut of resilient plastic sheet, using the techniques described in the section on scratchbuilding.

The punchings were fixed in place and, when hard, drilled 0.6mm to take stubs of 0.025in styrene rod to represent the cotters.

Door bar ends and cotters fitted.

A couple of well-used wagon interiors, clearly showing the battered appearance of the capping strips and clips. The wagon in the foreground was E136714 which features on page 24.

A finished wagon. Note the capping strip has been distressed to make it look battered.

A model of an LNER mineral with post-1936 lettering and small white stripe. This was hand-painted using matt enamel.

ABS

ABS produce cast whitemetal kits for the 1923 RCH standard wagon, the PO version being available with wooden end stanchions in 7-plank side-and-end-door, and side-door-only versions. They also produce kits for the LNER 8-plank and LMS 7-plank standard mineral wagons.

These have been available for many years, but, although beautifully mastered, they can look a bit heavy these days when compared to the finer detail on the more recent plastic mouldings. However, the castings are crisp and free from flash and with a little extra work they can be made up into quite acceptable models. Because of the nature of the material, the underframe parts, i.e. brake levers and V-hangers, are very heavy-looking, so I discarded all this. I also removed

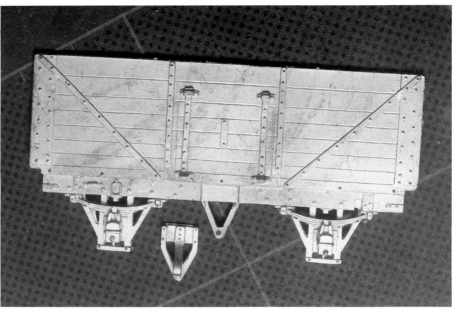

RCH 7-plank side-door wagon side as supplied.

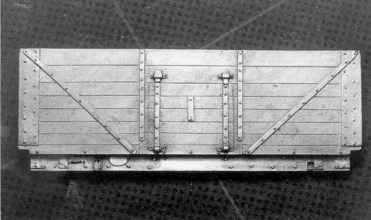

Left: *The side and end after removal of axleboxes and V-hangers and given a clean-up.* Right: *This is the result after filling the gap where the outside V-hanger fits.*

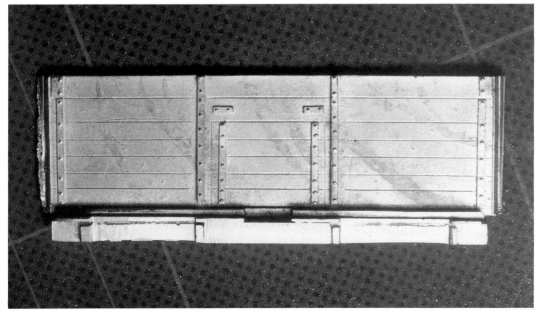

The inside of the solebars filed back to clear the W-irons.

Two door ends on the right as supplied, and on the left after removal of the cast door bar.

the cast-on axlebox/W-irons and replaced them with etched components.

I prefer soldering rather than using adhesives, at least for the main body. The joints can be done quickly and give a stronger result. I use a Carr's low-temperature iron which is specially made for use on whitemetal; this and his 70° solder and Red Label flux makes the job easy.

The first job is to remove the cast-on axlebox/W-irons and inside V-hangers from the sides with side cutters, then clean up with files.

The gap in the solebar where the outside V-hanger fits was filled in. I used the casting supplied for this after removing most of the detail. This was soldered into the gap and the face of the solebar carefully filed smooth.

A car body filler putty could be used just as well for a job such as this.

On the inside of the solebars I filed back the cast remains of the W-irons to allow room for the replacement etched components.

The cast-on hinge bar at the door end looked a bit clumsy and benefited from a tune-up. The bar was removed with a file, just leaving the tops of the vertical ironwork which form the hinges. These were carefully drilled 0.7mm dia to accept a new hinge bar made from 0.6mm dia brass wire.

Before assembling the body, I check the fit of the joints and give all mating surfaces a polish with a fibreglass brush

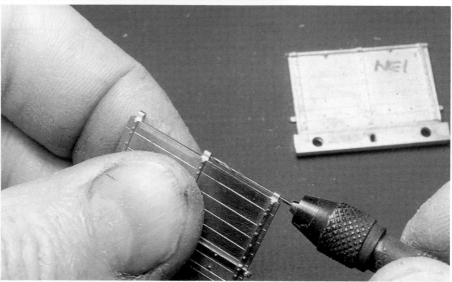

Drilling the eyes 0.7mm.

A new bar from 0.6mm brass wire temporarily in place.

Left: *Tack soldering a side and end together. Just make sure the parts hold together at this stage.* Right: *Adding the second side.*

Left: *This shows the body tacked together.* Right: *After final soldering, the joints should look like this. Most of the solder will flow into the joint if plenty of flux is used with a clean iron.*

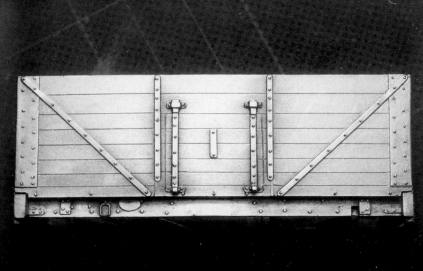

A finished body after cleaning up and the corners rounded off slightly. If the joint is a good fit and the solder has run right through, there should be no visible joint.

I find if the metal to be joined is bright and clean, the solder will flow through the joint easily.

Starting with a side and end, I hold the parts together with a finger and thumb and just tack them. It doesn't matter what the soldering looks like at this stage as long as it holds together. The other side and end were tacked on in the same way, then the body was checked for squareness and the close-fitting of the joints.

When all is well, the joints can be finished. I use plenty of flux and run the iron along the inside of each corner. The solder should flow right through the joint. Only use enough solder to fill the joint; we don't want a visible fillet inside the wagon.

The body was then given a thorough wash in warm soapy water to remove all flux residues.

The corner plates were carefully rounded with a fine file and emery board and the whole body given a polish with a glassfibre brush. The top edges were smoothed off as well.

I used 0.040in scribed styrene once again for the floors of these wagons. The LMS one had bottom doors and these were cut from the same material and let into the floor. The floors were glued in with 1-hour epoxy and left overnight to harden thoroughly. For additional strength, I fitted some extra pieces of styrene under the floor against the sole-bars and headstocks. These were fixed with superglue.

New floor made from Evergreen scribed styrene. This is described in the chapter on scratch-building.

Extra pieces of styrene fitted to strengthen the floor. The pieces behind the headstocks allow the buffer spring retainers to be fitted easily.

An LMS mineral from the ABS kit. This model has Exactoscale springing and modified ABS brakegear and axlebox castings.

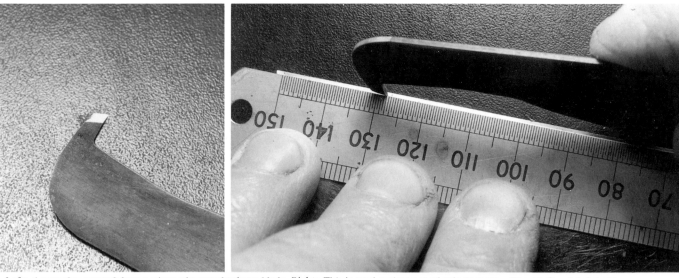

Left: *A scrawker ground from a piece of power hacksaw blade.* Right: *This is used against a steel rule to score a line on the nickel sheet.*

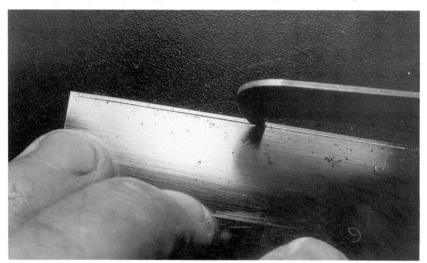

With the rule out of the way, the score is deepened until the strip breaks away.

I fitted capping strips and clips to a couple of these wagons to represent them in postwar condition. I was not keen on gluing these as I felt they would be too vulnerable to damage, so decided to make them from 0.005in nickel silver and solder them in place. I cut a supply of 0.005in x 0.030in strip using a scrawker; this is done on a hard surface, something like an offcut of Formica laminate or similar. This prevents any distortion of the metal which can happen using softer surfaces.

The strips were deburred by pulling them through a fold of silicon carbide paper a few times. I then tinned them on one side first with 145° solder, then on top of this with 70° low-melt. This is necessary as 70° solder will not adhere to brass or nickel-silver without tinning first with ordinary solder.

These strips were cut to the required length and deliberately distressed a little to represent a slightly battered look. Using the low-temperature iron, I just tacked them along the top edge of the sides.

The retaining clips were bent from some 0.5mm wide strip and fitted in the same way. The result was quite pleasing and well worth the effort. Buffers and couplings were fitted as described earlier.

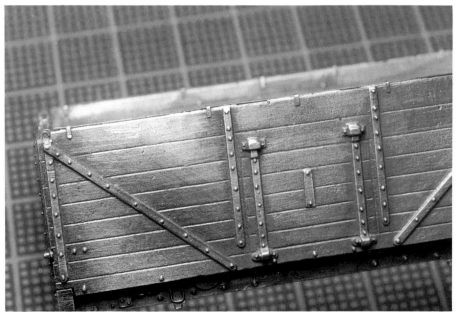

An LMS 7-plank wagon with capping strips and clips fitted. The strip only fits where it touches to give a battered look.

Left: This picture shows the bodies assembled and the end-door bars fitted. Right: *A 7-plank wagon with modified ABS brakegear and Masokits springing units.*

Three wagons built from the ABS kit. Both the NE wagons have compensated rocking W-irons. A gap is just visible above the right-hand axlebox. The Barnsley wagon should, I think, be an end-door wagon. It is lettered with POWsides transfers.

A selection of steel mineral wagons loaded with what looks like power station coal. Two slope-sided minerals feature in the foreground whilst the two wagons on the left clearly show the strengthening gussets on the top corners.

STEEL MINERALS

To round-off this section on kit-built vehicles, I decided to include three models from the Parkside range of steel mineral wagons. I only used the body and floor mouldings from the kits, replacing the solebars with Evergreen channel styrene and all the underframe with etched and cast components. The people at Parkside Dundas are very obliging and are quite prepared to supply parts from their kits if asked nicely.

The three wagons chosen were:

1. Dia. 1/100 slope-sided
2. Dia. 1/109 riveted body (built as Dia. 1/105)
3. Dia. 1/112 French type

SLOPE-SIDED MINERAL

On the whole, the body mouldings are first class, but can still benefit from a bit of extra work. I modelled this wagon in immediate postwar condition in bauxite livery with MOT numbering. These wagons had pressed steel doors, later to be replaced with welded types. As supplied, the side door mouldings look a

9,000 of these slope-sided wagons were built between 1944/7 to a Charles Roberts design. This wagon was pictured at Crewkerne in 1947 in bauxite livery which would have been carried until the early 1950s.
WESSEX COLLECTION

A model of a wagon similar to that shown above. Both MoT and MWT insignia were used.

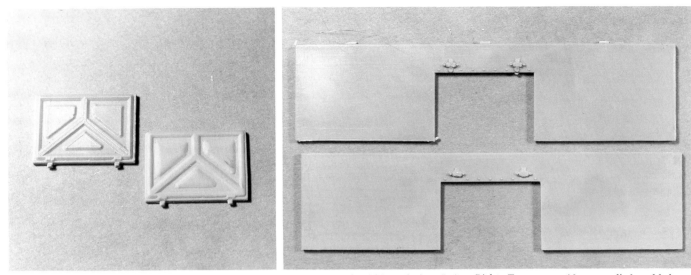

Left: *Side doors before and after modification. I also removed the moulded hinges before fitting.* Right: *Top, wagon side as supplied, and below with top door catches cut back.*

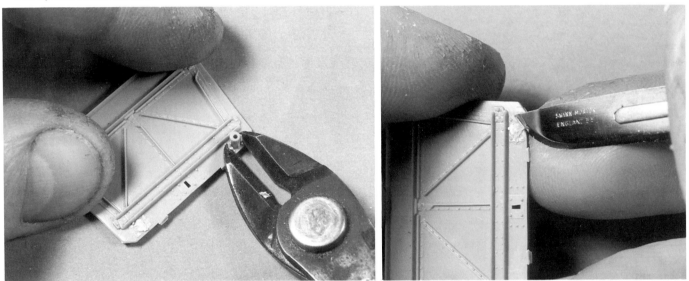

Left: *Removing the moulded buffers with cutters.* Right: *Finishing off with a No. 10 scalpel blade.*

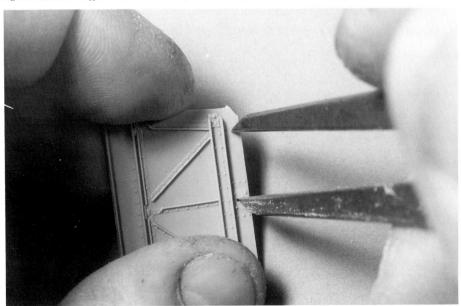

Marking buffer positions with dividers.

bit square-edged where in fact they should be more rounded to look like a pressed steel door.

I used a scalpel as a scraper to round off the detail on the door as much as possible and finished off with a fibreglass brush. I think the result is well worth the effort.

The wagon sides just needed smoothing with a fine emery stick to remove moulding marks. I also trimmed back the door catches which were replaced after assembly and fitting the doors.

The bulk of the buffer mouldings were cut off with Xuron shears, the rest being pared away carefully with a No. 10 scalpel blade. The buffer positions were marked at 23mm centres using dividers. I used ABS RCH 20in 4-rib buffers (FU09) for all these wagons.

The sides on these wagons are moulded in two parts, and it is worth taking care to get a good fit between the sections so that the finished side looks like one piece when assembled.

I took care to get the sides and floor exactly the same length, as these butt directly up to the ends. The ends were fitted to the floor first, followed by the top sections of the sides. This ensured that the top angles were level all round the wagon. The bottom sloping section was then adjusted to fit. It was approximately 0.5mm too wide so this was removed with a flat file until the side fitted flush with the bottom of the floor. The side stanchions and door were fitted next; the door needed adjusting a little so that it was also flush with the bottom of the floor. The bottoms of the door hinges were removed.

Body assembled. Note how the joint between the two parts of the side is almost invisible. The side door has been fitted with new top catches from 0.010in x 0.030in strip and bottom hinges from 0.035in styrene rod. Solebars are from channel styrene. The W-irons have been fitted at this stage to make it easier to locate solebar detail.

W-irons and brake gear fitted. This shows the cranked V-hanger. I have also started the solebar detail, whilst gussets between the side stanchions and solebar are already in place.

Strengthening gussets on the top corners from 0.005in styrene, on the left as fitted and on the right after fettling with a fine round file.

The strengthening plates on the top corners were made from 2.5mm squares of styrene fixed and left to harden before the inside radius was shaped using a fine round file.

I made new solebars from 1/8in channel styrene (Evergreen 264). This is excellent material for modelling steel solebars and gives a much finer appearance than the moulded ones supplied with the kit. It shows even more so on these slope-sided wagons as the solebars are flush with the side of the body and are more noticeable.

Before detailing the solebars, I fitted the W-irons and brake gear so the positions of the various rivets and plates could be

located easily. I used ABS FU08 brakes on all these steel mineral wagons. Once again this is all described in the relevant chapter.

The outside V-hangers (Exactoscale CW062 Type 1) are the correct cranked type for channel solebars and are drilled for 0.4mm wire pins. The V-hangers were stuck in place with a spot of superglue and drilled for the pins as described for the other wagons.

I used Exactoscale CW064 V-hangers for the inside ones. These are a true 'V' and missed the ends of the pins sticking through. On the real thing, both V-hangers would be held with the same bolts.

The wagon finished and ready for painting. The axleboxes on these wagons are modified MJT RCH type. The slot above the axlebox was filled in with epoxy putty and smoothed off when hard. I used Cuprinol 2-part wood filler.

This shows how I normally add weight to wagons using pieces of lead flashing sheet (from a builders merchant) glued in place to bring the weight of the model to approximately 50g, about 2oz, which I find is enough for compensated and sprung vehicles.

The finished wagon before being weathered. This shows up the solebar detail well.

The finished slope-sided wagon.

RIVETED MINERAL Dia 1/105, 1/109

This wagon was modelled in early condition, again in MOT bauxite livery. The only difference between the two diagrams is that the later Dia 1/109 no longer had bottom doors. The body mouldings are excellent and no modifications were made to them. The only additions were fitting grab handles to the end door and security chains from fine copper wire. Buffers were once again ABS FU09, and solebars and underframe exactly as the slope-sided wagon.

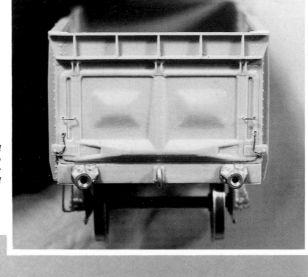

Diagram 1/105 steel mineral. New wire grab handles and chains have been fitted to the end door.

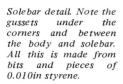

Solebar detail. Note the gussets under the corners and between the body and solebar. All this is made from bits and pieces of 0.010in styrene.

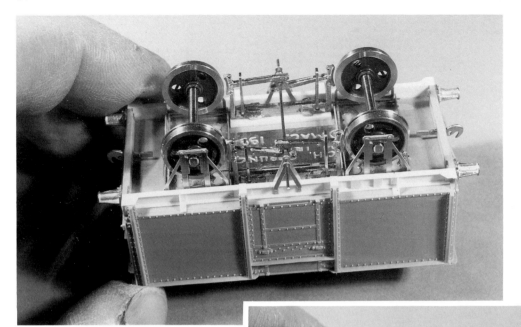

Underside showing Masokits W-irons. This also shows the different type of V-hanger fitted inside the solebar.

Brake levers and door stops fitted plus some more solebar detail. I have also fitted a bottom-door catch below the left-hand corner of the side door.

M.O.T. 54327
16 TONS

The wagon painted and ready for weathering and final detailing.

Both sides of the finished wagon. Note the different style of MOT and tare to the slope-sided wagon.

This wagon was built in 1948 to BR Diagram 1/103. These were riveted wagons, almost identical to the Diagram 1/105 wagon modelled but without the top flap. Note the pressed steel door; many were later fitted with riveted doors.

This picture shows a pair of the French type wagons amongst a selection of ex-PO wagons c.1960. They were not popular and caused several accidents due to the cupboard doors coming open. The lettering on the left-hand panel reads 'Not to be used for PW ballast or other engineers materials'.

J. H. MOSS

FRENCH TYPE Dia 1/112

This wagon was modelled in the condition in which it would have appeared in early BR days after refurbishment following their use in France during and after the war.

The body was assembled without any modification and the solebars and underframe details are as before.

These wagons had sheet tying-down rings on the sides and ends, although they began to disappear as the wagons got older. The base plates for these were cut from 0.005in x 0.5mm styrene strip and fixed to the body as in the photographs. I had to remove some rivet detail to fit these plates.

When these had hardened, they were drilled 0.4mm in the centre. I made the rings from 0.008in phosphor-bronze wire (Eileen's), wound tightly around a piece of 0.9mm dia brass wire to produce a little spring.

The rings were then cut from this with fine cutters.

This shows the base plates fitted for the tying-down rings.

The holding loops were made of fine copper wire from electrical cable. The rings were each slipped onto a short piece of this wire which was folded double and twisted to produce a little pin, and these were fixed into the holes with a spot of superglue.

I also fitted the grab handles below the buffers. (The slope-sided wagons which went to France in the war also had these handles.)

The door handles were replaced with metal ones from flattened brass wire and chains twisted from very fine wire fitted.

The finished wagon with rings fitted. I have also replaced the side door handles with ones from flattened wire and added a safety chain. Note the cranked brake handle to clear the body bracket. This means the lever guard is further towards the end of the wagon.

Left: *End view showing the tying rings and handles fitted below buffers.* Right: *This view shows the underframe fitted and a piece of 0.6mm wire passed through the inside vees in order to locate the outside vees.*

The finished wagon.

SOME CUSTOMISED EXAMPLES

The next six pages show a selection of prototypes, and models of them built from Slater's kits, modified to varying degrees to represent various prototypes, mostly as portraits of particular wagons. These show that the only way to achieve prototypical accuracy is to follow a period photograph. All these wagons are depicted as running in the 1940s or early 1950s. They were all built by Paul Karau who kindly allowed me to use them to illustrate this book. All the lettering was done by hand using a brush and enamel paints, and the results are, I think, quite remarkable, clearly showing what can be achieved by adapting and improving kits. He has written the following captions and describes his methods for lettering wagons on page 136.

Having built this Slater's 7-plank RCH wagon without end doors, I spent some time trying to find a postwar photo of a suitable prototype. The accompanying photos were the nearest match I had to hand, and all I had to do was to carve off the 'J' bottoms of the side knee washer plates adjacent to the side doors. I wasn't aware of any suitable transfers for this livery and although I hadn't tried hand lettering since I was a teenager, I decided to have a go, so this was my first attempt. Having seen the frighteningly impressive results which Alan Bracken- borough and Keith King have achieved, I am all too aware that mine is not perfect, but it captures the look I was after and satisfies my requirements, especially when weathered to match the pictures. The livery is red oxide with white lettering shaded black.

ROYE ENGLAND

ROYE ENGLAND

Similarly, the Peterborough wagon was a match to another wagon I'd already completed from a 7-plank RCH wagon without end doors. Again it was necessary to carve off the bottom of the side knee washer plates. This was my second attempt at hand lettering, and because I wanted to see if I could manage it, I did one side of this wagon before attempting the second side of the CWS wagon. The livery is medium grey with white lettering shaded black. All these wagons have Masokits springing and V-hangers, ABS brakegear and Ultrascale wheels.

From prototype photos, there appears to have been no end of variety within any train of coal wagons, so I wanted some variations on the Slater's kits. This 8-plank was made by cutting off the top plank from the RCH 1923 sides and ends and reducing the width of the exposed plank to match the five below. Before grafting on the new top pair, taken from a spare set of mouldings, these were also reduced in width. Of course, the diagonal side braces had to be carved off and replaced using thin Plastikard strip and individually applied nuts, as described on page 125. This model was based on the picture in Model Railway News *for July 1964 and hand lettered. The livery is red oxide with white lettering shaded black.*

Another Slater's 1923 RCH wagon matched to a prototype photo by carving off the bottom of the side knee washer plates. The model was inspired by the prototype picture below, but as I didn't have a photo of the other side, I thought I'd portray the full pre-war livery, which was grey with white lettering shaded black, and red corner plates.

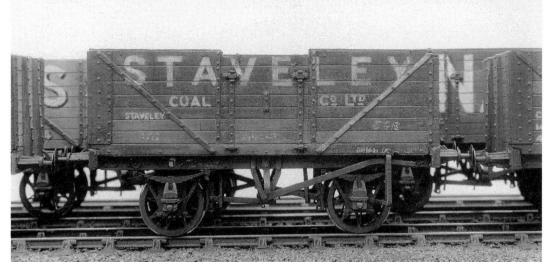

This Staveley wagon, one of my favourites, was inspired by the photograph below. Once again, the bottom of the side knee washer plates were cut away from the 1923 RCH mouldings and part of the top plank was removed to match the picture. It is painted dark grey (almost black) and hand lettered in white.

ROYE ENGLAND

Here is another example based on a Slater's RCH 7-plank kit, this time modified to represent a wagon with cupboard doors above the side door. It is unusual to see this on an end-door wagon, as photographic evidence suggests that most wagons with this feature were side-door-only types, which would normally have been unloaded by hand, thus allowing easier access to the wagon. A variant of the cupboard doors was a hinged top plank which lifted up and rested on the top of the wagon side.

ROYE ENGLAND

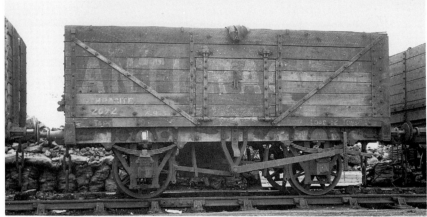

The 8-ton Amalgamated Anthracite Collieries wagon started out as a Slater's pre-printed Charles Roberts kit in the attractive Vauxhall livery. As I wanted postwar wagons, I thought I'd better find out when Vauxhall Colliery closed, and discovered that this happened in the late 1920s. I didn't know what to do then, until I discovered a wartime photograph featuring enough of an AAC wagon for a match to the kit. However, as the number was hidden from view, I gave it a likely-sounding one a few numbers away from a vehicle featured in Bill Hudson's *Private Owner Wagons* published by Oakwood Press.

The 12-ton wagon was inspired by the photo above. The diagonal side brace plates on Slater's 1923 RCH mouldings were carved off and replaced with the longer ones shown here. However, the axleboxes didn't match and as I didn't have any of the right pattern at the time, I gave it a number not far away from one illustrated in Model Railway News *for April 1939. Although this was cheating, the AAC fleet was so large that we will never find photos of more than a handful of them!*
ROYE ENGLAND

The Ocean wagon is another slight cheat. It started out as a Slater's pre-printed Gloucester 6-plank with a much earlier style of lettering which I didn't think would have survived until postwar years. It was therefore hand-lettered to resemble the accompanying proto-type photo. However, as the model doesn't match, it was given another number.

ROYE ENGLAND

Wheels at Burnetts wagon repair shops, Kettering, on 16th September 1952.   WESSEX COLLECTION

This shows how the real W-irons look on the inside.   WESSEX COLLECTION

UNDERFRAMES
ROCKING W-IRONS, SPRINGING AND BRAKEGEAR

When Protofour modelling began around 25 years ago, one aspect of the standards which caused controversy, and has done so ever since, are the pros and cons of the need to compensate rolling stock. I am not going to discuss this here, instead I will simply say that in 20 years or so of building models in P4 and other standards, I am convinced of the advantages of some form of compensation, equalization or springing incorporated into model rolling stock. The models described in this book incorporate the various forms of compensation/springing to illustrate the types available and their application. I will leave it to the reader to form his/her own opinion. It is something you need to try and experiment with yourself, and anyone who has not done so should not let themselves be deterred by some of the adverse comments made in the model press over the years. Don't believe everything you read, not even this!

The easiest way to incorporate compensation into a vehicle is a simple rocking W-iron system with one fixed axle and the other mounted in a rocking unit to form a three-point suspension, thus allowing all wheels to remain in contact with the track. There are several systems available commercially. Alternatively, these days there are springing systems which, although designed for the same purpose, have some advantages over compensation. They use a fixed axleguard system which enables axleguard tie-bars to be fixed more easily, and similarly brake lever guards can be rigidly mounted at the bottom as per the prototype. Finally, it is unnecessary to separate axle boxes and springs as in a rocking W-iron system.

However, for those modellers who prefer to build wagons with rigid underframes, all the following is still valid. Using etched W-irons and brakegear will greatly improve the appearance of the model as the heavy look of cast and moulded plastic parts will no longer be apparent.

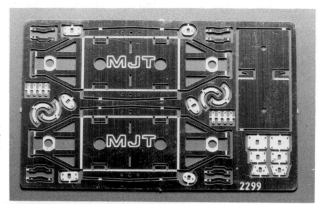

MJT W-irons. These also contain useful extra parts. This is the RCH/GWR type. BR types are also available.

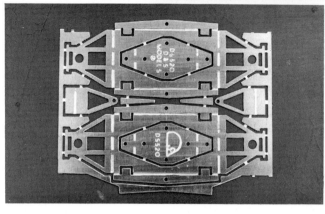

The D&S version. This is the RCH fret. Several pre-Group styles of W-iron are also available.

ROCKING W-IRONS

When the Model Railway Study Group introduced the first commercial P4 components via Studiolith, a rocking W-iron unit was among the items available. This was a pressed tinplate affair which, by today's standards, was fairly crude, but it did the job and there are probably many still around unused — we all bought too many. Soon the trade and specialist societies began to produce their own versions using etching technology, and it has to be said that some of these were less than successful, mainly because they were etched from material that was too thin.

Two currently available types which I have found very good are made by MJT Scale Components and D&S Models. They are both broadly similar; the MJT type uses a tab and slot system to provide the rocking unit, whereas D&S has a wire pivot, which in some ways is a more positive system. They are both well designed and etched in 0.015in brass to produce a robust assembly.

As with all compensated W-iron systems, provision will need to be made to allow one unit to rock. Some modellers prefer to separate the complete spring/axlebox from the solebars or use separate castings and fix these to the rocking unit, leaving a gap between the spring and solebar to allow for movement. I personally prefer to leave the spring fixed and separate the axlebox only and find this a less conspicuous method.

Both types used here are simple fold-up assemblies, and I like to reinforce the end folds with a fillet of solder. The bearings are fitted using a Paxolin jig (see Exactoscale springing, page 61).

All the wagons described in this book are fitted with Ultrascale wheels which I have found the best available. I always dismantle the wheelsets and reassemble them with Loctite 290, checking the back-to-back dimension with a gauge. This ensures that the wheelsets stay correctly set permanently.

Left: The MJT rocking unit. The baseplate has tabs which fit into slots of the W-iron and form the rocking pivot. *Right:* Here are both MJT units, with the fixed one on the left.

 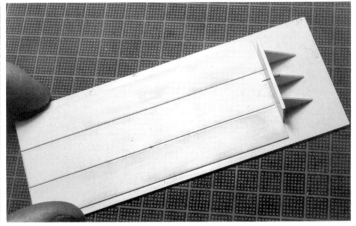

Left: The D & S version. The pivot is by means of a wire passing through the cradle and W-iron. I like these as they give a very positive pivot assembly. *Right:* This is the jig I use for checking the buffer height of vehicles. It is basically a piece of 0.60in styrene with the rest made up from 0.030in. The pin is for setting the height of Alex Jackson couplings which should be 10mm above the top of the rail.

The jig being used to check the height of the buffers. The top of the jig bisects the centre line of the buffer stock.

Before fitting any compensation units to a wagon, the buffer height must be checked and any adjustments made. I use a simple Plastikard jig to check this. Using a jig like this ensures all your stock has a consistent buffer height which is a significant contribution to reliable operation.

Before finally fitting the W-irons, check there is enough clearance between the solebars to allow the unit to rock (*Fig. 1*).

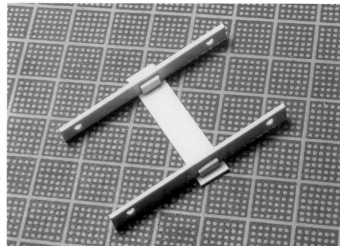

The little jig for setting the wheelbase of W-irons.

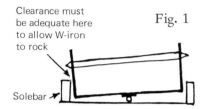

Fig. 1

Clearance must be adequate here to allow W-iron to rock

Solebar

When all is well, the W-irons can be fitted to the floor using superglue or quick-setting epoxy. I have another simple jig to set the wheelbase and ensure the axles will be parallel. It is easily made from scrap material, in this case .040in styrene, but make sure the holes for the axles are a close fit on the bearings.

The next stage is preparation of the axleboxes and springs. The wagons used to illustrate these units are ABS RCH LNER minerals. I used MJT LNER axlebox castings for them as it saved the trouble of cutting away the cast W-irons supplied in the kit. However, I will describe how the cast ABS axleguards were modified later, on another similar wagon, an LMS version using Exactoscale suspension (see page 64).

The jig being used to set D&S W-irons. The pivot wire is overlong and will be shortened and retained with a scrap of styrene later.

MAKING A W-IRON WHEELBASE SETTING JIG

This can be as elaborate as you wish. I used two 60mm lengths of approximately 6mm x 0.040in strip (this is not critical) and tacked them together with solvent at the ends. I drew a centre line and marked common wheelbase dimensions; I used 9ft, 10ft and 11ft. Do this as accurately as possible, then drill 2mm diameter holes at these positions, making sure the holes are drilled square as this can affect the parallelism of the axles. The two pieces can now be separated.

The jig is assembled around a set of prepared W-irons with bearings fitted. The important thing is to get the axles parallel and the W-irons in line. An easy way to do this is to stick the W-irons to a piece of graph paper with Sellotape, using the drilled strips as spacers.

When everything is nice and square, cross pieces can be glued centrally across the jig using odd scraps of styrene.

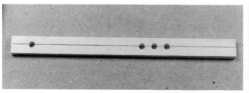

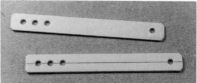

Left: *Two pieces of 6mm wide .040in styrene tacked together and drilled 2mm diameter at 9ft, 10ft and 1ft spacing.* Right: *The strips separated and the ends cleaned up.*

Left: *Assembling the jig. The drilled strips are fitted over the pin-point bearings. The W-irons are then taped down dead square to a piece of graph paper. Two strips of styrene are glued across the centre and allowed to harden.* Right: *The finished jig.*

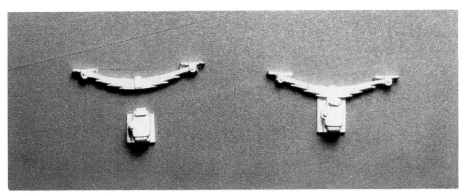

MJT LNER axlebox spring castings, showing, on the left, the axlebox separated to allow one end to rock. MJT supply these components separately anyway for this purpose, but at the time I only had the complete castings.

The axleboxes were separated from the springs by cutting with a fine piercing saw. Obviously this only needs doing on the rocking end. The springs could be soldered to the solebars, but in this case I used superglue and pinned the ends with fine wire pins, just to be on the safe side and prevent them getting accidentally knocked off later.

The top of the axlebox may need a little material removing to allow enough tilt on the rocking unit — ½mm up and down movement should be enough. These can also be fixed in place with superglue.

Left: *The springs and axleboxes fitted, illustrating the clearance necessary between axlebox and springs.* Right: *The result. Only about ½mm movement is necessary unless your trackwork is very bad.*

These pictures show that by separating the axlebox from the spring, the small gap required is not too noticeable. The brakegear is ABS, the safety loops have been replaced with strip brass, and etched D&S V-hangers used in place of the castings supplied.

Left: *I found the MJT rocking unit had rather more slop than I liked, so I fitted a strip of styrene each side to prevent this.* Right: *This is the D&S version. Make sure there is enough clearance behind the spring to allow the unit to rock properly. You can just see the pins in the end of the spring.*

This shows how the pin in the D&S rocking unit is retained with two scraps of styrene.

SPRINGING

EXACTOSCALE WAGON SUSPENSION

Exactoscale offer their own wagon suspension units under the title Fixed Axleguard Suspension System (FASS). As the title suggests, the axleguards are rigidly attached to the vehicle and the wheelsets slide in carriers behind the axleguards, suspension being controlled by a wire spring. It is not true springing whereby the wagon is actually suspended on the springs, but is probably best described as sprung-assisted compensation. As with all Exactoscale products, quality is first class, and, using the jigs provided, assembly is very straightforward. The instructions are excellent.

The axle bearings are parallel and made in phosphor-bronze whilst replacement axles are provided to convert pinpoint axles to parallel type.

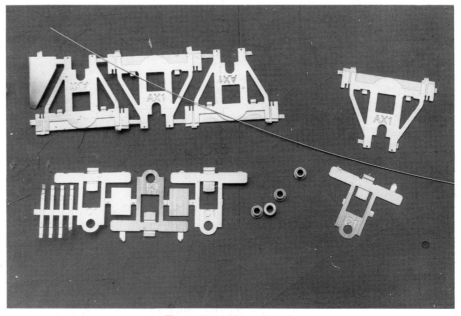

The separate axleguard version.

The units are available in two types, either separate axleguards which can be fitted to any desired wheelbase, or conversion units with a pair of axleguards and V-hanger as a single unit. These conversion units are available for most of the common wheelbases and current kits on the market.

They are supplied as a complete set of parts for one wagon, consisting of axleguards, spring cradles, bearings and spring wire. The system is designed so that with the wagon weighted correctly, the bearings just sit in the tops of the axleguard slots. Any undulation in the track allows the springs to depress the corresponding wheel and so keep it in contact with the rail.

The components are etched in 0.010in brass which, for normal rocking W-irons with pin-point axles, would be rather too thin. With parallel axles, no outward pressure is exerted on the axleguards so this is quite adequate. The parts can be easily distorted when cutting out. For this and most other etched components

I therefore use a little home-made cutter ground up from a piece of power hacksaw blade. This is used on a piece of spare laminate, i.e. Formica, but any hard surface will do.

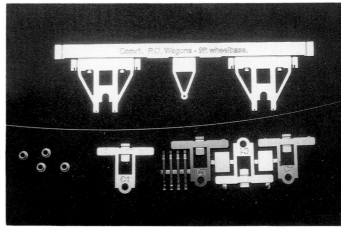

A conversion unit for 9ft 0in wheelbase PO wagons.

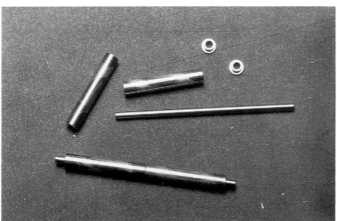

Left: *The parallel axle conversion set, showing axle bearings, components for one axle and a finished axle.* Right: *Here they are fitted to Ultrascale wheels. They can be used with any 2mm bore wagon or coach wheels. The axles are assembled using Loctite 601.*

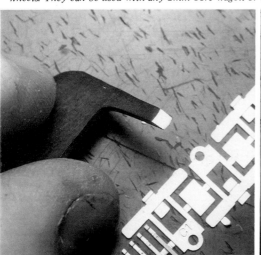

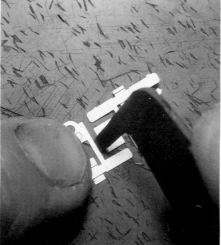

Left: *The tool used for cutting etched parts.* Centre: *The tool in use.* Right: *I find using a tool such as this enables etched parts to be removed cleanly and with no risk of distortion.*

Before assembling the cradles, I have found it best to fold-up the axleguard units first to check the fit of the spring cradle between the spring anchors. It may be necessary to ease the ends of the cradles to allow them to slide easily between the spring anchors. This is easier to do than when the springs are fitted.

The instructions recommend the use of 188° solder paint (Exactoscale MA013) to fit the bearings and springs to the cradles and this is fine. I actually used 145° solder and Carr's Green Label flux, and this worked just as well. It is important to use the minimum amount of solder as any reaching the outside face of the cradle could prevent the unit sliding properly. Wash off any flux residues completely before assembling the cradles into the axleguards.

Soldering an axle bearing into the cradle. It is supported on a piece of Paxolin with holes drilled in it.

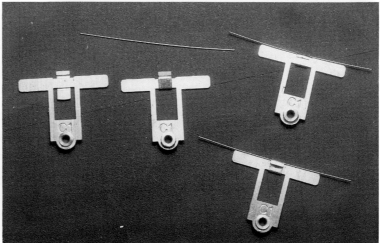

Left: *This is the result. Keep the solder to a minimum to prevent any reaching the outer face of the cradle.* Right: *Fitting springs to the cradles. The wire is cut to be approximately 4mm longer each side of the cradle. The cradle on the left shows the two tabs at the top which are to locate the springs. The next one has the bottom tab bent up, the spring fits in the groove above this. The cradle on the top right shows the spring in place with the top tab bent over to locate it. And finally, bottom right, the tabs are soldered to retain the spring. Here again I used 145° solder for this job.*

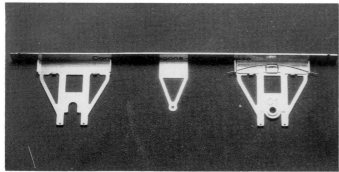

Left: *Here we have an axleguard unit with one cradle fitted to illustrate the assembly. The spring clips into the two outer tabs and the cradle is pushed down onto the small tabs. This only illustrates the components; the cradles are not fitted until the axleguards are fitted to the wagon.* Right: *The outside face. When the wagon is ballasted to its correct weight, the bearings should just rest in the tops of the slots with the springs compressed.*

Fitting the axleguards to the model is made very easy with the setting jigs supplied by Exactoscale. These automatically set the axleguards at the correct spacing and ensure the axles will be square. With the axleguards assembled in the jig, the whole assembly can be transferred to the wagon and glued in position. Alternatively, a piece of brass sheet can be soldered across the two and this then enables etched brake gear, etc., to be assembled away from the wagon. Exactoscale supply etched wagon floors for this purpose, but personally I prefer to build the wagon with a permanently fixed floor and make the underframe separate when using these units.

Once again the underframe details are described in a separate chapter.

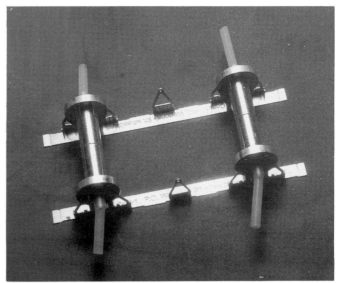

Here the axleguard units are assembled on the jigs. The spacers between the axleguards have a rod through them which fits the bearing slots. These are held in place with small pieces of neoprene tube – very simple.

Left: *And here is the assembly test fitted to a wagon, in this case an ABS mineral.* Right: *The units fitted with a piece of brass, thus forming a removable unit . . .*

. . . and to allow brakegear to be built up before fixing to the wagon. In this case, the brakegear is by Masokits. I prefer to solder the brakegear to the floor rather than using glue for a job such as this. The wagon is an ABS LMS standard mineral. Also notice how little the bearings project from the face of the axleguard, making it necessary to remove very little from the back of the axlebox – very useful with small axleboxes. The axleguard tie bars are fitted last with a spot of superglue.

A bit of a posed picture to demonstrate end-tipping a wagon at Slough Gas Works. A pity the end door was still closed. This view also clearly illustrates the gap between the brake push rods, which sometimes had wood packing fitted between them.

Removing cast W-irons. An ABS axlebox/spring casting.
Right: Removing bulk of W-iron with side cutters . . .

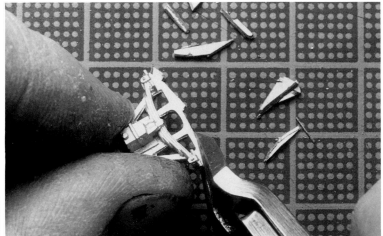

Left: . . . to achieve this. Right: The rest is removed
with a fairly coarse flat file.

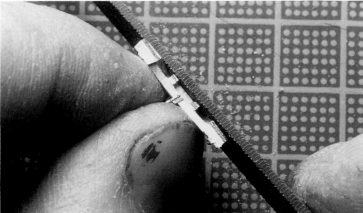

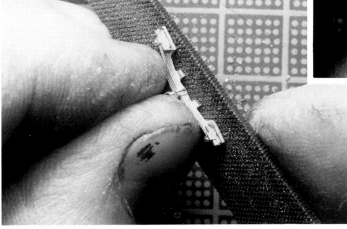

This is the result.

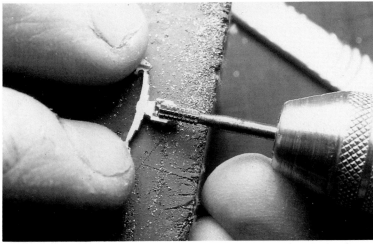

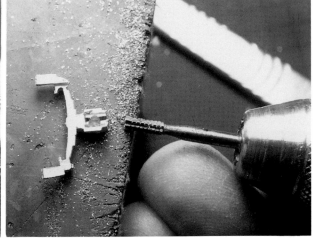

Using a burr in a mini-drill to cut a slot to clear axle bearing. This is an MJT casting but the method is the same. Alternatively, one could use a
round file and simply file a groove across the spring and axlebox.

MASOKITS W-IRONS

These are a fairly recent development and offer modellers the only true springing system for wagons, i.e. the vehicle is actually suspended on the springs, allowing wheels to rise and fall. The etched brass W-iron units are similar in appearance to conventional rocking W-irons and accommodate etched stainless steel springing units which carry the pin-point bearings.

The kits are supplied with a wheelbase setting jig which covers wheelbases from 8ft to 12ft. An additional jig is available for wheelbases up to 25ft, which also has provision for 6-wheel underframes. Two types of springs are available to cater for 3ft and 3ft 6in wheels.

The wheelbase setting jig is a mixed blessing; it is fine if the kit you are using is moulded with an accurate wheelbase dimension, otherwise it is not much use. However, there are ways around this, as we shall see. If the kit is accurate, this jig does make assembly easier.

Preparation of the W-iron units

The W-irons are pinned to the setting jig with 1/32in brass wire to locate them accurately while soldering. Before folding up the W-irons, check the holes in the jig and W-irons are a close fit on the wire pins as any slop here can affect the squareness of the axles. Use a taper broach if necessary to ease the holes, and, when all is well, remove any burrs with an emery stick. It is easier to do this with the units in the flat. I have also found it an advantage to remove the etch cusp in the corners before folding to ensure there is nothing to prevent the units coming out square.

Next fold over the tie bars. I find it easier to do this before folding up the W-irons. Grip the W-iron in a pair of smooth-jawed pliers and bend over the tie bar against a piece of Paxolin or wood covered in fine wet and dry paper. This avoids any chance of slipping which can happen if you just use a plain piece of material. I use this for all small parts in etched kits which require folding. Finish the fold with pliers to crimp them up tight. They could be secured with solder or even superglue but I haven't found this necessary.

The W-iron can now be folded up. Using the Paxolin block, fold the ends

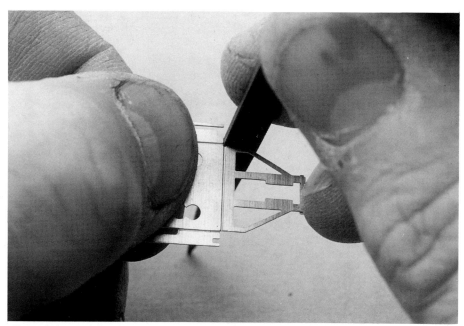

Removing etch cusp on W-iron before folding. Only a few strokes are necessary here with a fine needle file.

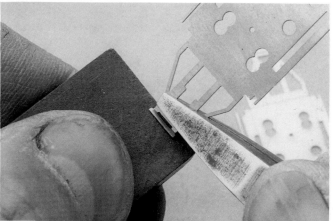

Bending over the tie bar against a piece of wet-and-dry-covered Paxolin.

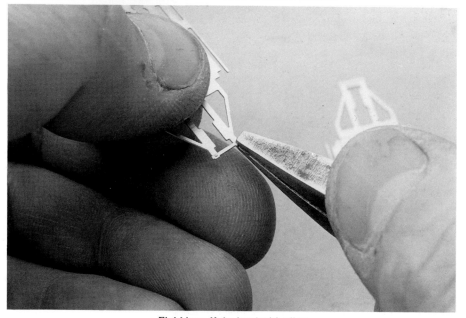

Finishing off the bend with pliers.

first and go just past 90° and then fold the sides. Folding the units so the legs bow in slightly gives you the opportunity to adjust them out should the axles be too tight.

The folds at the ends at least are best strengthened with a fillet of 145° solder; keep the solder clear of the inside face of the W-iron. Now wash off all traces of flux. Should the axleguard need tweaking to adjust end play on the axle, the soldering will not prevent this.

When Mike Clark first introduced these W-iron units, it was subsequently found that due to variations in the depths of various makes of pin-point bearings, it was not always possible to eliminate side play. To overcome the problems with deep bearings, he introduced an etch of stepped washers which fit between the bearing and spring carrier to allow different depths of bearings to be used. The etch also incorporates a gauge to measure the depth of the bearings and determine the desired washer permutation. I have made quite a number of these sets to date and have found that the following method gives consistent results. After trying several sources of bearings, I found the best by far are made by

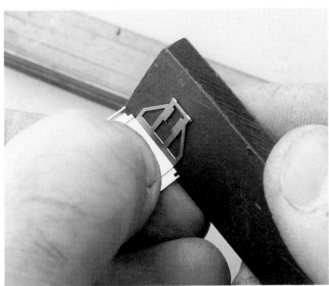 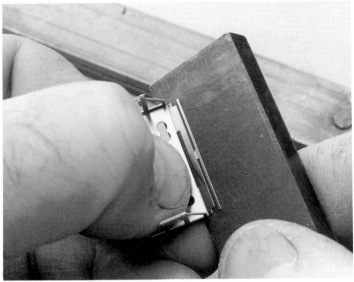

Left: *Forming the end of the W-iron using wet-and-dry covered block* . . . Right: *. . . followed by the sides.*

The W-iron folded up. This shows the legs bowing in slightly and the benefit of relieving the corners before folding. I have found it necessary to shorten the spring retaining bar slightly at each end to allow it to clear the legs.

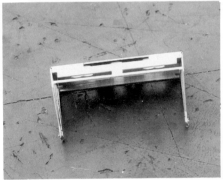 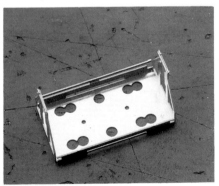

 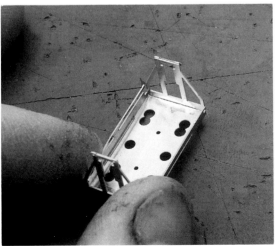

Left: *Applying a fillet of solder to strengthen folds.* Right: *No more than this, though.*

Exactoscale. They are produced in phosphor-bronze and are of consistent quality and depth of pin-point. I still use the packing washer and set them all for the tightest position. If the axle then comes out too tight, the W-irons can be tweaked out or I even reduce the points of the axles a little without any detrimental effect on the running. I have standardised on this approach, which has been totally satisfactory for me (see *Fig. 2*).

The bearings cannot be soldered in to the stainless steel springs using normal fluxes. Carr's Brown Label flux is recommended and works well with 145° solder. I find it helps if the parts are brightened up with a fibreglass brush first. This flux is evil stuff, very strong with powerful fumes, so take great care when using it and allow good ventilation. Thoroughly wash the parts in clean water afterwards. I've found it best to prepare about a dozen or so sets of springs at a time to save going through this messy job each time I build a wagon.

The bearings are best fitted using a piece of Paxolin or hard wood as a support with holes to take the bearings. Plenty of flux and a clean iron does the job easily; make sure the solder flows all round the bearing. Stainless steel is not a good heat conductor, so if the iron is taken away too quickly, the solder may not penetrate the joint properly. Don't breathe in the fumes! I suppose the bearings could be fitted with superglue.

I haven't tried this myself but if you don't like soldering, it may be worth a try.

Before separating the springs from the fret, the bearings must be reduced in depth to minimise their projection through the W-iron, which in turn reduces the amount of material needed to be removed from the backs of the axleboxes to clear the bearing. A little jig is included with the kit to assist with the filing.

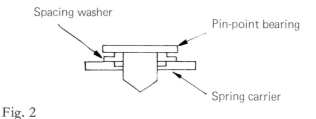

Fig. 2

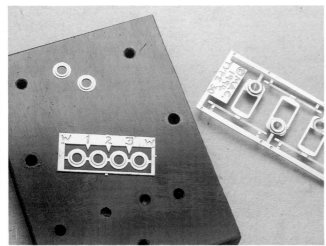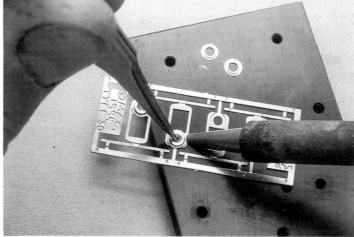

Left: *These are the adjusting washers which fit behind the bearings.* **Right:** *Soldering in the bearings on a piece of Paxolin drilled with holes to clear bearings.*

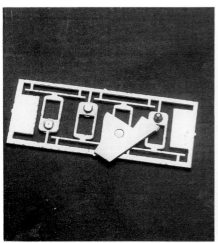

Left & Centre: *The filing jig in use to reduce the depth of the bearings.* **Right:** *Filing chamfer on the bearings.*

Before finally separating the springs, a small chamfer is filed on each bearing to allow a little more clearance in the axlebox. The springs are separated by simply breaking the fret between each one. This just leaves a piece of fret attached to the top of the spring which must be cut away. I use Xuron micro shear cutters for this job. Ensure any burrs left after removing springs are filed away, otherwise

this could prevent movement of the spring in the W-iron.

Finally the spring is bent at right-angles to the bearing carrier and a spot of solder put in the bend to strengthen it.

If you are going to use the wheelbase setting jig, the W-irons can now be fitted to it.

I only put a small dob of solder each side of the setting jig first, then remove

the wire pins before finishing soldering. The pins are only there for location and don't need to be soldered in.

FITTING MASOKITS W-IRONS

These units differ from conventional rocking compensation units in that because the W-iron units are fixed, there is no need to separate axleboxes and springs from the solebar. Of course, separate axlebox spring castings can be used but they can still be fixed to the solebar or W-iron, only requiring a clearance at the back for the bearing to rise and fall. Another benefit of fixed W-irons is that axleguard tie-rods and brake lever guard stays can be rigidly mounted. The foregoing is equally applicable to the fitting of Exactoscale FASS W-irons.

For this example, I am fitting the Masokits suspension to a Slater's 1923 RCH mineral wagon. These kits have accurately spaced axleboxes to scale 9ft WB so the wheelbase setting bar can be used. The axleboxes and springs remain attached to the solebars and only the moulded W-irons need be removed. The bulk of this I removed with a scalpel, using a modified No. 10 blade like a chisel, on a cutting mat, to remove most of the moulded W-iron. Used in conjunction with a standard No. 10 blade, it is an excellent combination for carving plastic mouldings, etc.

Having cut away the bulk of the moulding, the remaining bits can be filed off flush with the back face of the solebar. A good sharp, fairly coarse file is best for these jobs. Then with a pointed blade, the remaining bits of W-iron and ragged edges can be removed. I normally have four or five scalpels on the go at any one time which saves having to keep changing blades.

Before fitting the solebars to the wagon body, the backs of the axleboxes need opening out to allow the wheel bearings some up and down travel. They can be carefully carved away with a scalpel, but I prefer to use a small burr running very slowly in a mini drill. Only use this method if your drill can be run slowly, i.e. it has a variable speed transformer. If you try to do this with a fast cutter, more than likely the plastic will just melt. Obviously, only remove enough material to clear the bearing. Check as you go, using the W-iron unit.

It is worth checking that the solebars both match each other. Very often

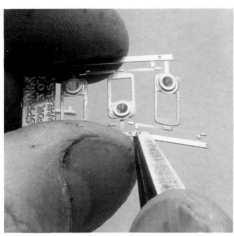 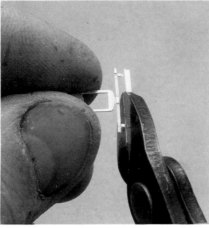

Left: *Breaking the springs from the fret.* Right: *Trimming remaining fret from spring. Don't cut off the small tabs on top of the spring.*

 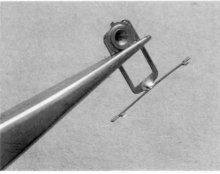

Left: *Folding over the spring.* Right: *A small bead of solder in the fold strengthens the bend.*

Fitting the W-irons to the wheelbase setting jig.

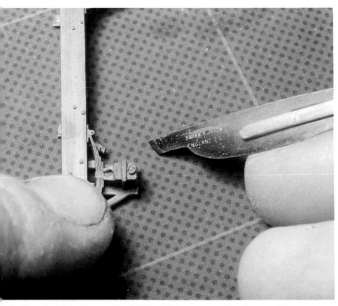
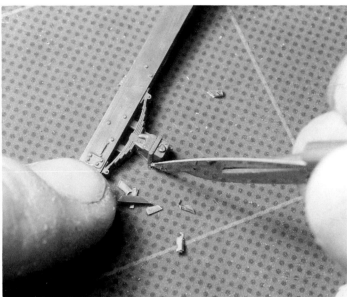

Left and right: *Removing bulk of W-iron moulding from solebars.*

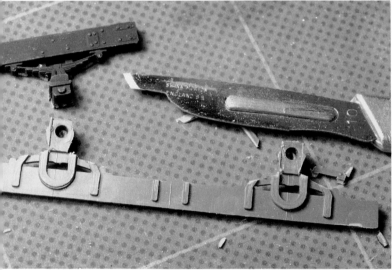
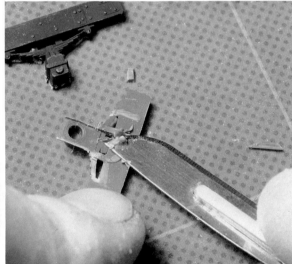

Left: *Removing W-irons using modified No. 10 scalpel blade.* Right: *and removing the bits at the back with an ordinary No. 10.*

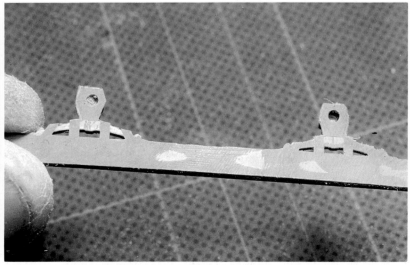

Left: *Using a good sharp file to remove remaining W-iron moulding, support axlebox against your finger like this to prevent it being broken off the spring.* Right: *It should then look something like this.*

Left: *Use a sharp pointed blade to clean up after filing.* Right: *To produce this.*

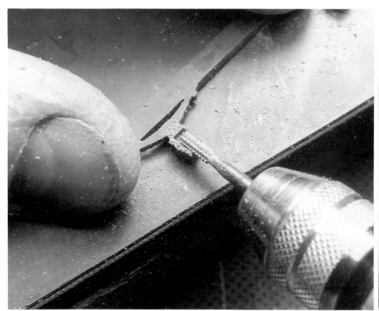 

Left: *Using a small burr in a mini drill to remove material from the back of the axlebox. The drill must be running slowly and use little pressure.* Right: *This is the result.*

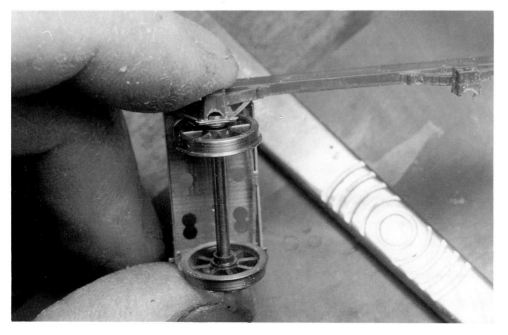

Checking clearance of bearing in axlebox. This shows the reason for chamfering the bearing, so reducing the amount of material needed to be removed from the back of the axlebox.

the mouldings in kits are not mirror images of one another and by lining up the axleboxes, the ends of the solebars do not match. This is easily remedied and helps to ensure the axles will be square. With these springing units, there is not much room for error, and if the axleboxes do not correspond with the bearing, binding can result. When all is well, the solebars can be fitted using the W-irons to position them.

It is worth pointing out that these springing units are 25mm wide instead of the normal 24mm of other W-iron systems and allowance must be made for this when fitting the solebars.

It is not really necessary to use the wheelbase setting jig to position the W-irons and, in any case, if the mouldings in the kit do not incorporate an accurate wheelbase, it is no use. In such cases the W-irons can be fitted as separate units as with any other W-iron system. Alternatively, the jig can be used with one W-iron only soldered and the other end adjusted to fit the axleboxes. However, I have found the central bar of the jig a useful mounting for a brass plate which can be used as a base for assembling etched brakegear, as described in the next chapter.

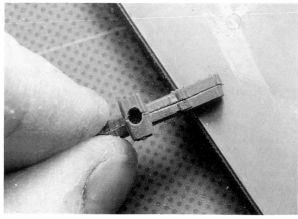
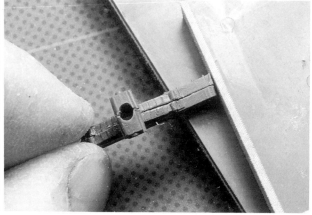

Left: *Showing how the two solebar mouldings do not match each other by lining up the axleboxes. It can be seen that the ends of the solebar are slightly different.* Right: *Filing the ends flush with each other to ensure the axles will be square when the solebars are fitted.*

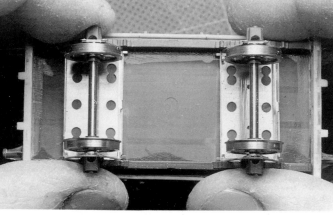

Left: *Solebars have been fitted with W-iron units in position but not fixed at this stage. Before everything hardens off, check that the springing works freely.* Right: *The W-irons being fitted without the wheelbase setting jig.*

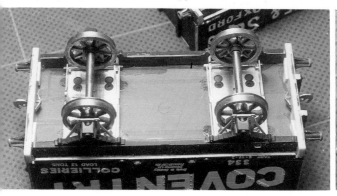

Left: *Once the position is correct, the W-iron units are glued to the floor with 5-minute epoxy or superglue.* Right: *The small brackets are for mounting Alex Jackson couplings.*

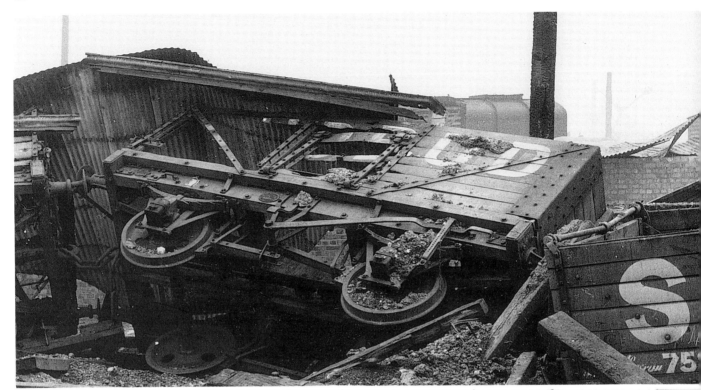

Two pictures of wagons damaged during air raids in the Second World War. The top picture shows a Judbud RCH 1923 7-plank wagon with much of the side sheeting blown away. This clearly shows the arrangement of ironwork and washer plates. The Stephenson Clarke wagon in the bottom picture illustrates a ratchet brake lever guard. Note also the ends of the internal diagonal ironwork on the solebars. Both pictures show clearly the wood blocking between the brake push rods.

BRAKEGEAR

Having got the wagon onto its wheels, the rest of the underframe detail can be fitted. This is the area where most plastic and whitemetal kits fall down. If the parts of the kit for these components were produced to scale thickness, they would be much too fragile. In the majority of kits, the body components are excellent but the underframe can look rather chunky and lack the fineness of the real thing. This is not intended as a criticism of the kit manufacturers who frequently offer an excellent product at a competitive prive. If they were to supply a super-detailed kit with additional metal parts, the price would then be prohibitive. What they provide is a good basis for those of us who like to spend the time improving them. Fortunately, there are many after-market accessories available to tempt the modeller who wishes to take this approach, i.e. buffers, axleboxes, springs and brakegear.

Whilst it may be possible to modify some parts to improve their appearance, I prefer to discard most of the underframe and replace it with metal components. In particular, brake levers and V-hangers are obvious candidates for replacement, either using etched components or making them up from scratch.

For the actual brakegear, the Masokits range offers what is possibly the state-of-the-art in etched brake components, covering most of the popular types of wagon brakegear plus additional components to cater for many variants and different wheelbases. These parts are not everyone's cup of tea, they are time-consuming and rather fiddly, but for those who enjoy this level of modelling, the effort can be very rewarding and the results look superb. Similar etched components, i.e. brake shoes, hangers, push rods, vees, etc, are available from Exactoscale and Ambis Engineering.

An alternative for those who perhaps prefer something a little more user friendly and less time-consuming is the excellent ABS range which offers a good selection of brake parts. Worth a little fine-tuning, these can look very good, as I hope to demonstrate on two Slater's wagons, an RCH 1923 7-plank and a Gloucester 5-plank.

Both these wagons have Masokits sprung W-irons fitted without the wheelbase setting bar. As the brakegear will be glued to the wagon floor, a brass sub-floor is unnecessary.

The brakegear units are ABS FU08 (RCH independent 4-shoe brakes) modified by removing the cast safety loops. I like to use a sharp scalpel to pare away the bulk of the unwanted casting, finishing off with a fairly coarse needle file. The file will become clogged, but this is unavoidable when filing whitemetal. It can easily be cleaned with a piece of brass used as a scraper across the teeth. The action of scraping will produce a serrated edge on the brass which in turn will clean out the teeth. Also ensure that the hole in the centre crank will accept 0.6mm wire.

The new safety loops were made from approximately ½mm wide strips of 0.008in nickel silver cut from the sheet using a scrawker made from a piece of power hacksaw blade.

The brake shoe assemblies can now be tried on the model. It may be necessary to trim the shoes to clear the wheels, and this is also done with a scalpel. The brakes may need some packing on the underside of the floor to get them in the correct relationship with the wheels. I use

Using a piece of scrap brass to clean a file clogged with whitemetal.

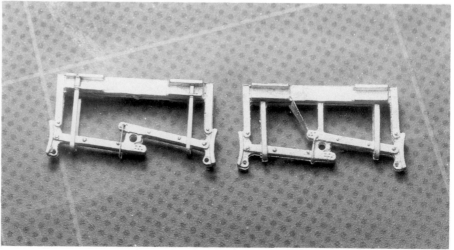

ABS brakegear, shown as supplied on the right and as modified on the left. The cast safety loops have been replaced with ones from nickel silver strip and the brake push rod safety loop is from 0.008in phosphor-bronze wire fitted into a drilled hole in the end of the top rod.

The modified brakegear in position and showing the styrene packing and also how the brake shoes have been pared away at the back for clearance.

Here the inner vees have been fitted threaded onto a length of 0.6mm brass wire. The centre section of the rod between the brakes will be cut out when the model is finished.

a V-hanger held on the outside of the solebar in the correct position, and make sure the pivot hole in the brake assembly will line up. In this case, a strip of 0.040in styrene did the job. When all is well, the brakes can be held in position with a spot of superglue. This sticks very quickly and saves having to hold everything by hand while epoxy cures. If any adjustments are required, the joint is easily broken and repeated. When everything is OK, a good dob of epoxy can be run into the joints to finally fix them. I use 1-hour epoxy for this as it gives a good working time before it starts to cure.

The V-hangers are fitted next. First a length of 0.6mm brass wire is passed

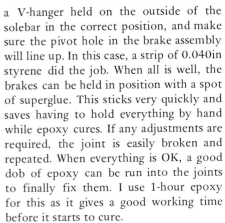

RCH V-hangers from D&S Models. The half-etched dimples are drilled 0.4mm for wire pins.

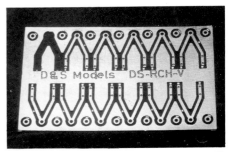

The Gloucester version from Masokits.

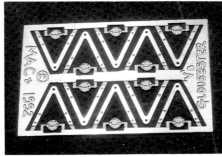

The Gloucester wagon complete and ready for final finishing. The pins holding the V-hanger can be seen.

through the cast cranks in both brake assemblies. The inner V-hangers are then threaded on and superglued to the back of the solebars.

The outside V-hangers are first drilled 0.4mm through the half-etched dimples before fitting. This allows them to be pinned for additional strength, the pins representing the holding bolts. For the RCH vees, I used D&S components whilst those for the Gloucester wagon came from the Masokits range.

The brake levers and guards for these two wagons are from the Ambis Engineering range. The lever guards are not available at the time of writing, pending re-design. They are etched in 0.007in nickel silver and are very fragile. Masokits now supply brake levers, guards and V-hangers separately.

HOME-MADE BRAKE LEVERS AND GUARDS

If you wish to improve the appearance of a wagon but retain most of the brakegear, just replacing the brake levers and guards with metal components can dramatically improve the model's appearance. It is not difficult to fabricate your own parts for those items.

BRAKE LEVERS

I use 0.010in nickel silver for these. First cut off a strip about 40mm wide. This allows for a little extra length in the levers. Using a scrawker, cut off strips approximately 1.25mm at the wide end, tapering to about 0.75mm.

These are deburred using a home-made emery stick, made from a piece of thin strip wood, like an ice-lolly stick, with silicon carbide paper stuck on with double-sided adhesive tape.

Here is the completed 1923 RCH wagon. The etched parts have been chemically blackened prior to final painting and weathering.

Cutting lever blanks from 40mm wide strip of 0.010in sheet. They are longer than is necessary but it is easy to make them fit the wagon.

 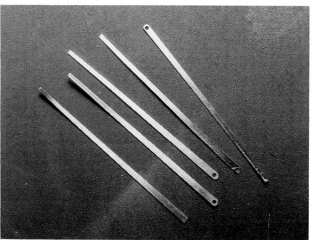

Left: *Cleaning up and deburring the levers using home-made emery stick on a rubber-faced block to prevent slipping.* **Right:** *Here are some part-finished levers, ends drilled and rounded off.*

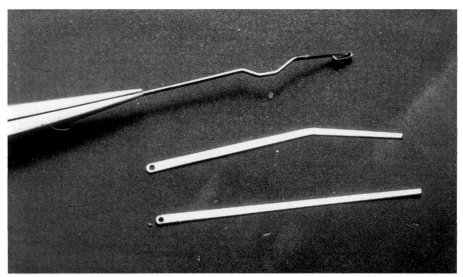

Stages in bending the levers. The crank is put in first and the final bending to shape done against the wagon to get the bends in the right place.

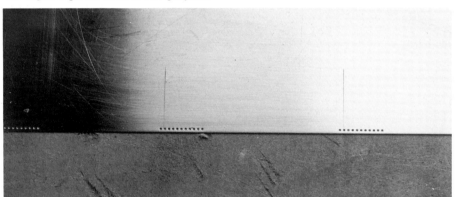

First stage in making lever guards. Impress groups of rivets approximately ½mm in from the edge of the sheet, about 1 inch apart. A strip is then cut off the sheet with a scrawker, leaving the rivets in the centre of the strip. Do as many as you're likely to need.

A 0.6mm hole is drilled in the wide end of each lever and the end rounded off.

The levers are best bent to shape after the lever guards are in place, to ensure getting the bends correct. The crank in the lever can easily be bent in the flat, using pliers.

LEVER GUARDS

I use a rivet impressing tool to represent the row of holes in the lever guard. I know they can be drilled, but back-to-front rivets make life much easier. The idea is to use the riveter to impress a row of dimples in the guard to represent the pin holes. After all, we are only creating an impression and, in any case, from anything more than a few inches away, they are all but invisible.

I mark off lines approximately 1in apart at right-angles to the edge of a piece of 0.010in nickel silver sheet, about 6in long. I then impress about ten or so rivets starting from these lines, spacing them approximately ½mm apart and ½mm in from the edge of the sheet.

The strip is cut off the sheet using a scrawker and again the burrs are removed with a wet-and-dry stick. Apart from improving the appearance, the wet-and-dry also removes the sharp edges which the scrawker produces.

Bending these guards is easily done using a little jig made from 0.040in styrene or brass if you prefer.

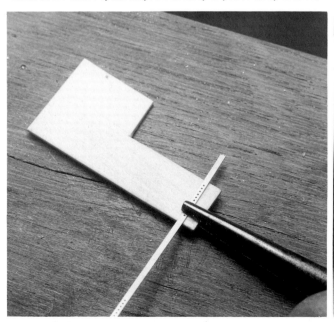

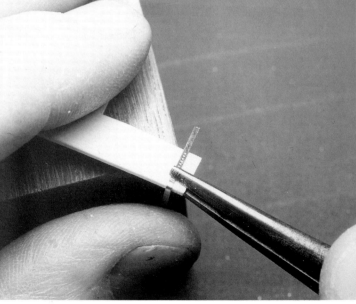

Left: *Prepared strip held on a small styrene jig for bending to shape. The bottom edge of the jig is rounded off.* Right: *The bottom bend of the guard being bent round the bottom of the jig . . .*

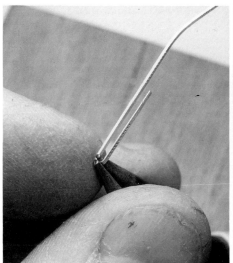

Left: . . . to produce this shape. Centre: *The top of the guard has both legs bent at right-angles using the jig as a guide.* Right: *The first bend looks like this.*

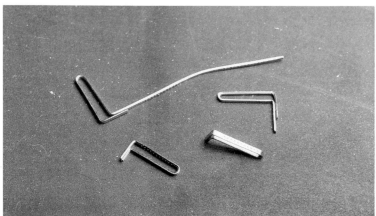

Once the bends are finished, the two ends are soldered together and trimmed off to produce the result shown on the bottom left. The lever guard is then glued into a hole drilled in the solebar.

This shows the result on an ABS LNER mineral wagon with lever and guard both in place. The door stop is also from 1mm wide nickel strip, drilled and pinned using 0.4mm wire as per the V-hangers. The pins are secured with Loctite 290. I've also added a safety loop to the end of the brake push rod using 0.008in phosphor-bronze wire.

MASOKITS BRAKEGEAR

Modellers who enjoy a challenge and like to incorporate as much detail as possible should relish the Masokits finely etched parts for complete wagon brakegear. These kits include all the parts needed to build super-detailed brakegears, including V-hangers, brake levers and guards.

The range covers many of the common brakegears found under freight rolling stock of the steam era plus many supplementary parts for variations. The instructions supplied are very comprehensive.

The instructions suggest gluing some parts to the wagon floor and this is fine if you like this approach. I prefer to build the brakegear onto a brass sub-floor and use solder assembly throughout. I find this easier, quicker and stronger, although with this sort of modelling, strength is relative.

The example shown here uses Masokits sprung W-irons with a piece of brass soldered to the wheelbase setting jig. This allows the whole underframe to be built up as a separate unit before fitting to the wagon. The same method can be used with Exactoscale FASS units or even standard rocking W-irons.

Before separating the components from the fret, I like to drill all the holes first. The instructions suggest using brass lacemaking pins to assemble the joints in the brakegear. In my experience, these are too thick and require too large a hole in some of the components, leaving them rather weak. I use Duchess pins which have a shank diameter of only 0.45mm. These also have a much smaller head, which, when fitted from the inside, is almost invisible.

Duchess pins and a large range of other brass and nickel-plated pins are available from D. J. Hornsby, 25 Manwood Avenue, Canterbury, Kent, CT2 7AH. Tel: 01227 454605. The catalogue number for Duchess pins is A11/Q 17 x .45 brass.

The holes in the V-hangers and brake levers are drilled to take 0.6mm wire. When this is done, I deburr all the parts by rubbing the fret with a fine emery board, then remove the parts as they are required. Some are very small and easily lost.

The inside V-hangers are fitted first. I use Carr's Green Label flux and 145° solder for all this type of work. This flux is strong stuff but, provided the parts are washed thoroughly after each modelling session, no problems have been found.

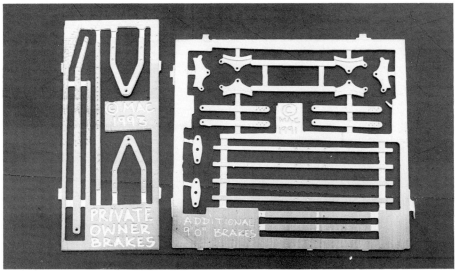

The 9ft wheelbase PO brakegear.

Left: *Fitting a plate between W-iron units on which to build up brakegear.* Right: *Here the inside V-hangers are fitted. Make sure they are central between the wheels, otherwise the brakegear will not fit correctly.*

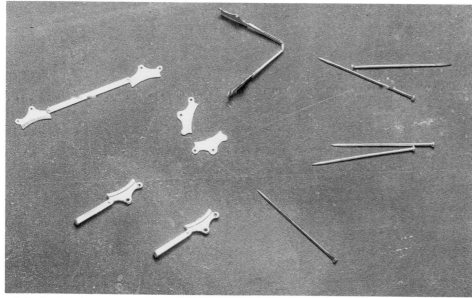
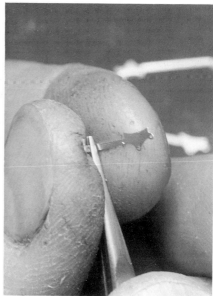

Left: *Brake hangers and shoes with completed items at bottom left. The Duchess pins are also shown here.* Right: *First stage in bending the brake shoes. A stout pair of tweezers is best for this job.*

I usually keep a small jar of water handy when soldering small assemblies and give them a dip after each operation. This also keeps things clean and prevents flux residues building up on the work, hands and tools.

Brake hangers and shoes are folded up using a stout pair of pointed tweezers and then soldered with the packing piece between the shoes. Make sure the holes in the shoes for the push rods are clear after soldering.

The completed hangers are now soldered in place, carefully lining up with the wheels. Make sure there is enough clearance for the wheelsets to move up and down and clear the brake shoes as the springs operate.

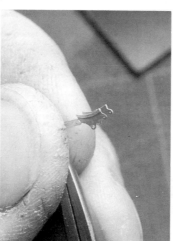
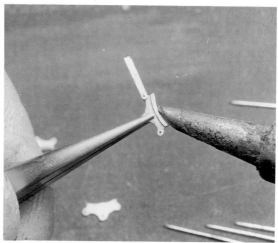

Left: *Make sure the shoes come together square.* Right: *Finally soldering them together. The packing pieces go between the shoes.*

Soldering the brake hangers into position.

The cranks are next, which are double thickness. They are threaded onto a length of 0.6mm wire which can then be soldered to the vees, but do not solder the cranks yet.

The next job is to prepare the push rods, which can be assembled with or without the blocking between the rods. This was wood on the real thing. If blocking is fitted, it makes assembly a little easier as the push rods are then in one piece. This wagon has separate ones which makes it a bit more of a fiddle.

The ends of the rods which connect to the crank need drilling, and a series of half-etched holes indicate various positions. On the real thing, the variety of holes allowed adjustments for wear to be made. To determine which hole needs drilling, fit the push rod to the brake shoe with a pin and bring the end of the rod and crank together. It is then easy to see the relevant hole position. Only do one push rod assembly at a time and fix each one as you go; trying to do them all at once is a nightmare.

Assemble the two ends of the push rods with pins fitted from the inside. It may be necessary to shorten the one through the crank as the V-hangers might get in the way. When all is well, a little dab of solder will secure the joints. Only use a minimum of solder but use plenty of flux to wet the joint right through.

This will ensure the solder will flash right through the joint. Now repeat this for the remaining three push rods.

Once all the push rods are assembled, the pins are trimmed off on the outside, leaving them a little bit proud. They can be filed flat but still leaving a little above the surface. The heads on the inside cannot be seen. Ordinary wire could be used just as well, but the head of the pin just makes things a bit easier; they can only fall out from one side!

The safety loops can now be fitted. After folding up, they are simply cut to length and soldered to the mounting plate.

The underframe has to be fitted to the wagon now before the rest of the brake-

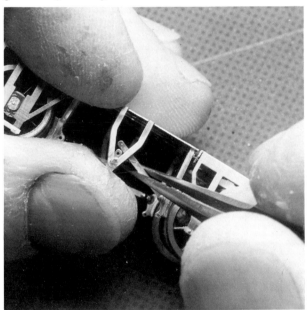

Left: *Brake hangers in place and cranks threaded onto 0.6mm wire between the V-hangers.* Right: *Test fitting the brake push rod to see which hole position to use.*

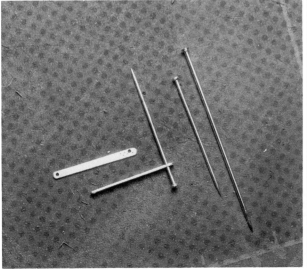

Left: *The push rods are then drilled to take a Duchess pin. This shows how close the hole is to the edge of the rod. If lace pins are used, the hole would break out. A lace pin is shown on the right to illustrate the difference.* Right: *The push rods being fitted, pinned from the inside. The centre section of the pivot rod will be removed once everything is complete.*

Left: *Push rods all fitted and joints cleaned up. The worst is over!* Right: *Here the safety loops are fitted. This assembly is now fitted to the model before the rest of the brakegear can be finished.*

Left: *The underframe is fixed in place and the outside vees glued to the solebar with a spot of superglue. Leave this to cure for half an hour, then drill holes for 0.4mm wire.* Centre: *Holes drilled for 0.4mm wire pins. This strengthens an otherwise weak joint and looks better too.* Right: *Pinning the outside V-hanger. The wire is secured with a spot of Loctite 290.*

gear can be completed. I use 5-minute epoxy to secure it. Once the glue has cured, the outside V-hangers are fitted. These should be drilled 0.4mm for wire pins before fitting. The vees are held in position with a spot of superglue. Leave these for half an hour or so and then drill through into the solebar 0.4mm.

The wire pins are secured with a spot of Loctite 290 which I prefer to the usual 601. It is much thinner and penetrates the joint better. When this has cured, after about 5 minutes, all traces left on the outside must be wiped off as paint will not stick to it.

The pins are trimmed off and left just proud of the vee to represent the holding bolts.

The pins are trimmed off and cleaned up. I think this picture clearly shows the delicacy of this brakegear.

Brake lever guards are a simple little fold-up job and are superglued into 0.7mm holes drilled in the solebar. An advantage of having fixed axleguards is that the bottom lever stays can be rigidly fixed to the guard and W-iron, thus giving extra strength here. These were made from a piece of scrap etch from the brakegear fret. They are easier to fit if they are made overlong and trimmed off after soldering in place.

The brake lever is soldered to the pivot and really needs fixing to the lever guard. I soldered mine but it is rather tricky; maybe gluing is a safer option or even assembling the lever and guard before fitting. Masokits also supply door springs on a separate fret and these are what I used here.

Above: The lever guards folded up and ready to fit to the model. Right: These are glued into 0.7mm holes drilled in the solebar, as shown here.

Fitting the bottom stay between the lever guard and W-iron. Make these longer than necessary, as it gives something to hold onto while soldering.

These have to be soldered, in this case with the plastic axlebox and spring in situ, so be careful. Plenty of flux and a quick dab with a hot iron does the job.

Brake lever fitted.

The underside; the centre of the brake shaft has been removed.

Masokits door springs.

. . . and finally the Masokits door springs fitted.

This chapter describes the methods I use to scratchbuild wagons from Plastikard. I find this an ideal medium for wagon building, being easy to cut, file and join together. Only a few simple tools are needed and these have been listed earlier. I do, however, make use of simple jigs and other bits and bobs to make life easier, and these are described as I go along.

Some may question the need to scratchbuild when some excellent kits are available. Well, kits are not made for every type of PO wagon and it is often easier to scratchbuild than modify existing mouldings. Apart from this, I enjoy scratchbuilding, and, of all the models built for this book, these have

given me the most satisfaction. This is what modelling is all about for me.

All the wagons described here were made using Slater's and Evergreen products and these have proved totally satisfactory.

FLOORS, SOLEBARS, HEADSTOCKS
For open wagons I usually prepare the floor first, then fit the solebars and headstocks. This gives a strong flat base on which to build the body. To begin then, the first job is to cut out the floors. These are made from Evergreen 4080 scribed styrene, the same as I use for the floors of the kit-built wagons.

To determine the size required, the outside dimensions of the wagon body need to be known. In the case of 1923

RCH wagons, they are 16ft 6in x 8ft (which in 4mm scale becomes 66mm 30mm. For older wagons, one can o work from known dimensions. I example, the Gloucester Carriage a Wagon Company official photograp give inside body dimensions, so allowan need to be made for the thickness body planking (side sheeting). On r wagons this was 2½-3in thick, so for models I use 0.040in styrene. Where body dimensions are available, it usually possible to work out the wid and length fairly accurately by work from known dimensions such as position of buffers and axleguards, e Many of the older pre-1923 wagons w

SCRATCHBUILT WAGONS

One of the wagons described in this chapter — a scratchbuilt model of a 1923 RCH 7-plank lettered with POWsides transfers.

A lovely photograph which illustrates the variety to be found in private owner wagons and shows some of the differences which would be difficult to reproduce from kits. The Handel Kilvert 7-plank could be built from the Slater's Chas Roberts kit but the diagonal ironwork would need replacing. The Slater's kit has curved ends to the vertical ironwork similar to the TW wagon next to it, but the wide top and bottom planks would make that one a definite case for scratchbuilding. Similarly, the Stephenson Clarke wagon, with its slightly wider bottom plank and two odd top planks, would need scratchbuilding. The Jacksons wagon appears to have been a standard 1923 RCH 8-plank design, which would be possible with the ABS kit. The LMS wagon was one of the conversions from a mineral wagon to merchandise traffic. Note the gap in the top plank and higher door. It looks as though it would be possible to build the other Stephenson Clarke wagon from the Slater's Chas Roberts 7-plank wagon kit, whereas the Thorncliffe wagon again has a very wide bottom plank. This just gives a small example of the differences to look for when studying PO wagons. Finally, the old 4-plank wagon on its own to the right of the picture clearly shows the pivoted type end-door securing bar. This picture was taken at Yarnton on 17th July 1942. NATIONAL RAILWAY MUSEUM

Here is a wagon that can only be modelled by scratchbuilding. It was a 4-plank wagon which had been extended by the addition of three planks. Note the original diagonals and corner plates. The doors appear to have been replacements.

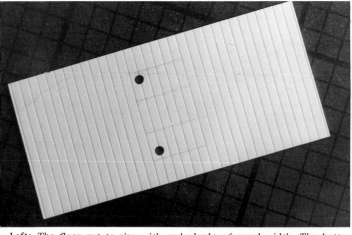 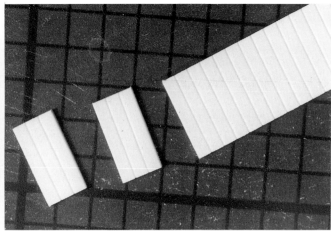

Left: *The floor cut to size with end planks of equal width. The bottom door positions are marked and a hole drilled to take a piercing saw.*
Right: *Bottom doors cut from a 12mm wide strip of floor material.*

Left: *Removing the bulk of the door aperture.* Right: *Cleaning up the door aperture with a fine flat needle file.*

built to customers' individual requirements and body sizes varied considerably.

So once we know the body size, the dimensions of the floor can be deduced. Almost without exception the floors on wooden-bodied mineral wagons were the same length as the body over headstocks. They fitted between the side rails, so the width of the floor is less by the amount of twice the side rail thickness.

I use 0.030in x 0.080in (Evergreen 134) for side rails, so for the 1923 RCH wagons, the floors can be cut 66mm x 28.5mm, which is 1.5mm (0.060in) less than the body width of 30mm. Because the scribed sheet is not exactly correct for the prototypical floor plank spacing, I centralise the floor so the widths of the end planks are the same.

If the wagon is fitted with bottom doors, I cut these from the same material as the floors. Because of the incorrect plank widths, this gives a slightly undersized door. The only alternative is to scribe the planking by hand, but for this application I can live with the error.

Bottom doors fitted and straps added.

To make the doors, a strip of floor material is cut 12mm wide, to represent 6 plank widths. I make the doors 3 planks wide, and these are simply cut off the strip using the plank lines as a guide.

The positions of the doors are marked on the floors; on the real thing they were usually 2ft 0in apart. A hole is drilled to allow a piercing saw to be used to cut out the bulk of the door aperture. I find this better than using a scalpel which tends to distort the floor. The apertures are cleaned up with a flat needle file until the doors are a good fit in the holes.

When all is well, the doors are fixed with solvent and two little strips of 0.005in x 0.030in are added to represent the straps.

The Gloucester Carriage & Wagon Co's workshop, in 1924, with RCH 1923 underframes being assembled. The side and end knees and side rails can be seen fitted in place on one of the

I prepared and fitted the headstocks and solebars next. These are made from 0.060in x 0.156in strip (Evergreen 157). If the model is of an older narrow-bodied type, it may be better to use 0.040in thickness for the solebars to allow room for W-iron units. Most of the etched rocking type W-iron units are 24mm wide, as are those of the Exactoscale springing system, whilst Masokits sprung W-irons are 25mm wide.

When fitting rocking W-iron units, a little extra clearance must be allowed to let the unit rock; about 0.010in each side should be enough.

I fit the headstocks first, flush with the end of the floor, making them slightly overlong to allow for the thickness of the side rails which are fixed to the edge of the floor. The headstocks are trimmed back after the side rails have been attached.

The solebars are fitted next, making them a good fit between the headstocks and not forgetting to allow room for the chosen W-iron system.

I make the side rails from 0.030in x 0.080in (Evergreen 134). The ends of these are cut to fit around the ends of the headstocks and I have made a little jig to support the end when filing these steps as unsupported they are a bit fragile.

The jig is made from a strip of 0.060in styrene with another strip of 0.040in material stuck on top.

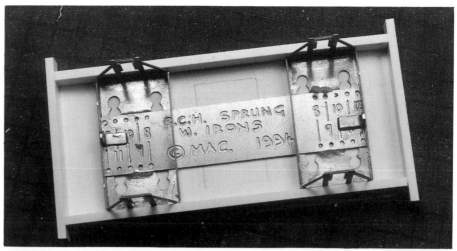

Floor with headstocks and solebars, with a Masokits W-iron unit test fitted.

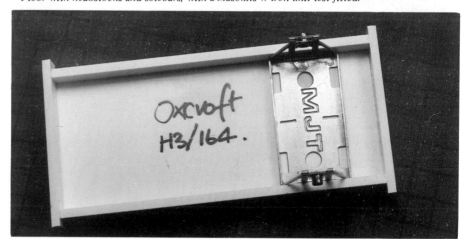

This time with MJT rocking W-irons.

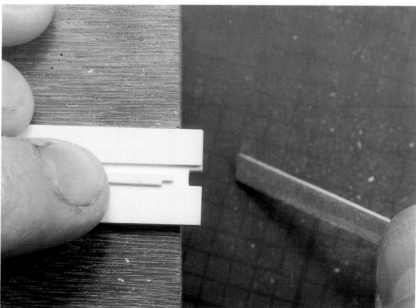

Jig used to support side rails when filing the ends.

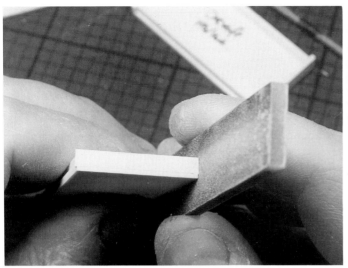 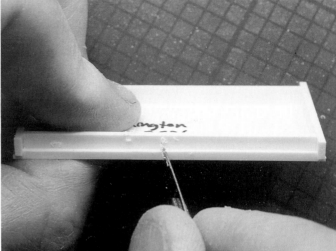

Left: *Trimming the headstocks with an emery stick.* Right: *Bottom of side rail being chamfered with a scalpel.*

Left: *A finished floor/frame assembly.* Right: *Using an eraser to declog an emery stick.*

Take care to get a good fit around the headstock, the side rail must be flush with the top of the floor. After these are fixed in position, the ends of the headstocks are trimmed back and smoothed off flush with an emery stick.

The bottom edge of the side rails of some wagons were bevelled slightly and this can be done on the model by scraping with a scalpel.

I find emery sticks excellent for working on styrene and keep a few just for use with plastic; they stay clean this way. Once used on metal, they will always leave dirty marks. In due course, they will get clogged with dust, but this can be removed easily with an ordinary pencil eraser.

Buffers and couplings could be fitted at this stage but I leave these until I have finished the bodies.

BODIES

The next stage is preparation of the sides and ends, for which I use 0.040in styrene. This is slightly overscale but not enough to worry about. The plank lines are scored using a home-made tool ground up from a broken power hacksaw blade. This keeps its edge forever. A tool made from ordinary steel would be quite satisfactory and should keep its edge for a fair time if only used on plastic.

The first thing is to determine the plank spacing for the chosen model. Many PO wagons used standard width planks, or 'sheeting', to be correct. Early wagons used odd sizes and combinations of planks and a certain amount of guess-work is necessary to work out the sizes.

The common plank widths for later wagons with their scale equivalent in inches is as follows:

$8\,^7/_8$ in = 0.120in
$8\,^3/_8$ in = 0.113in
$7\,^3/_8$ in = 0.099in
$6\,^7/_8$ in = 0.093in

Knowing the scale sizes required, I used a standard vernier caliper to accurately mark the plank positions. For those unfamiliar with using a vernier, a dial caliper may be a better option as the dimensions are read direct from the dial.

I prefer to work with a full-sized sheet of styrene using the short side, which is usually around 220mm long. This allows plenty for two sides and two ends of a wagon. Make sure the edge is straight, cutting a new one if necessary. This edge will become the top of the wagon side.

Using the RCH 1923 7-plank wagon as an example, these wagons had two top planks $8\,^7/_8$ in wide and five bottom ones

Left: *The depth gauge end of a vernier caliper used for marking plank positions.* Right: *The tool for scoring the plank lines.*

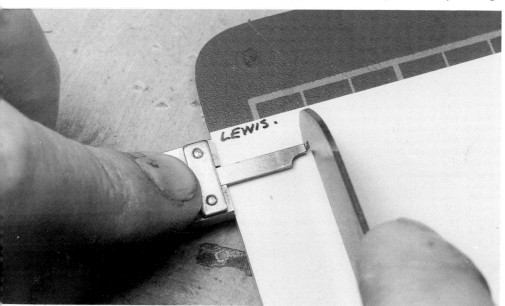

Marking the positions of plank lines.

6 7/8 in wide. The settings for the vernier, working from the top, would be 0.120in, 0.240in, 0.333in, 0.426in, 0.519in, 0.612in and 0.705in.

So, for the first plank, set the vernier to 0.120in and, using the depth gauge at the end, make a mark with the scoring tool at each end of the sheet. Do this on both sides, i.e. inside and outside planks. Now repeat this for the second plank at 0.240in and so on until finished, marking all the plank positions.

The lines are scored with the aid of a 12in steel rule, taking care to keep exactly to the marks and only pressing lightly, taking several strokes each time.

When all the lines are scribed, the side can be cut from the sheet by scoring the

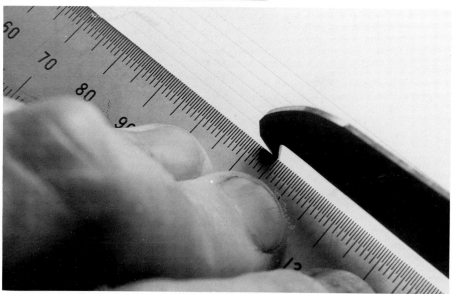

Scoring the lines against a steel rule.

Using a fine emery stick to remove any burrs.

After a brush over with a glassfibre brush, the result should look like this.

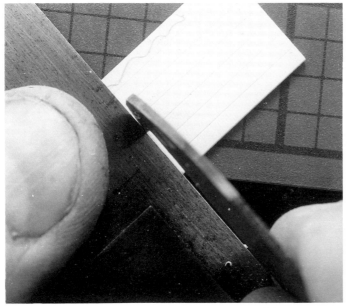

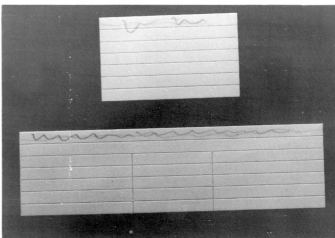

Left: *Scoring the door positions using a small square.* Right: *A side and end ready for assembly. Pencil marks indicate the top edge.*

This picture shows the side aperture cut out. It was cleaned up with a fine file (see opposite). Note also the 'London' top plank.

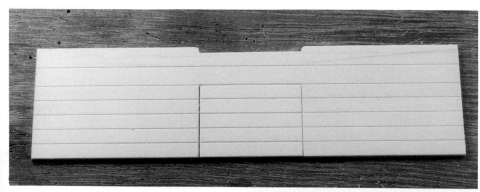

New door from spare body strip fitted into aperture.

bottom plank line both sides with a scalpel and snapping off the strip. Making the side and ends in one strip ensures that the planks will line up all round the body. I give the sides a gentle rub over with a fine emery board to remove any burrs and finish off with a fibreglass brush to clean out the dust from the grooves.

It is worth going over the grooves with the scoring tool very lightly to clean them out. I also mark the top edge lightly with a pencil to avoid getting them mixed up after cutting out the parts.

Sides and ends are cut out next. The ends fit between the sides, so are cut 0.080in less than the width of the floor including side rails. This must be done carefully to ensure the sides, when fitted, will be flush with the side rails.

I cut the sides slightly overlong and trim them to length after fitting. Before assembly, the side door positions are marked using the scoring tool. Side doors were normally 4ft 0in wide but varied in height to match the plank widths.

I modelled one of these wagons with the side door open to show a wagon being unloaded. Before assembling the body, I cut one side-door aperture out with a piercing saw and made a new door from a spare piece of the scribed body strip. This wagon also had the so-called London top plank, which had the centre of the top plank reduced in height above the side door. I believe this was done to satisfy a local problem concerning the height of wagon sides when hand loading. On the model I reduced the height by 1mm.

The main body can now be assembled. I fix one end in place flush with the head-stock and central on the end, i.e. equal amounts of floor at each side. A side is fixed in place, making sure the side door is central; the plank lines on the floor help here. I use a small engineer's square to ensure the end is vertical. The other end and side are then fitted and left to harden thoroughly.

The body assembled. The door was fitted after all detail was finished.

Body during assembly. Note how sides overlap to be trimmed off. Check side is central in relation to floor planks.

Using a square to ensure end is upright.

A photograph taken in the mid to late fifties, when there were still a fair number of ex-PO wooden wagons in evidence, most of which were getting pretty rough. This shows how the bodies became distinctly bow-sided.

Most wooden-bodied mineral wagons developed a distinct bow in their sides as they became older. I have tried several ways to achieve this in the model, either physically bending the sides before assembly or forcing them apart with pieces of styrene and leaving them for some time in the hope they will stay bowed, but I have not found any of these methods very satisfactory.

The following method I believe is the answer, some of these models were made over the course of a year and they have remained stable so far. I simply force out the body sides to the required amount with a couple of pieces of 0.040in styrene and then immerse the whole body into near-boiling water for a moment or two

Forcing out the sides with scraps of 0.040in styrene.

then cool it under a cold tap. This has the effect of heat-forming the body to the desired shape and de-stressing the styrene at the same time.

This only works with models built with Plastikard; don't be tempted to try it on kit-built wagons as these use a different type of plastic, which will soften and distort, leaving a hopeless mess.

The excess material at the ends is trimmed off with a scalpel, then smoothed off with an emery board. I round the corner slightly at the fixed end of the wagon to allow the corner plates to fit tightly around the end. These will have a slight radius in them, as we shall see.

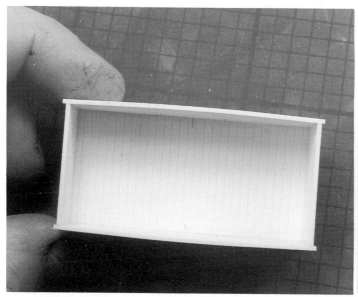

Left: *After a few moments in near-boiling water, the result is this.* Right: *Trimming off the surplus from the ends.*

Left: *Smoothing off and rounding the corners slightly with an emery stick.* Right: *The result.*

On wagons with end doors, I scribe plank grooves on the visible ends of the wagon sides, using the plank-scoring tool.

The headstocks can be drilled now and the buffers and hooks fitted exactly as described for the kit-built wagons.

When fitting buffer stocks, I slide lengths of 1mm rod approx 3in long through the castings as a visual aid to their alignment. This helps to ensure the buffer stock is square in the headstock.

Wooden end stanchions on mineral wagons were normally 5in square, tapered towards the top, although there were variations on this, particularly on older wagons. I make these using 0.063in x 0.063in strip (Evergreen 8606).

On real wagons, they were normally set at 2ft 9in centres, so I have made a

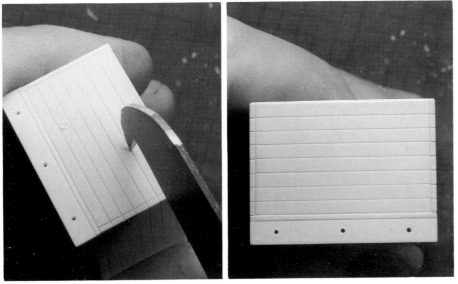

Using the plank scoring tool to scribe the plank ends at the door end of the wagon.

Left: *Opening out the buffer holes with a round file. This is rotated counter-clockwise.* Right: *Countersinking the holes slightly to allow buffers to fit tight against headstock.*

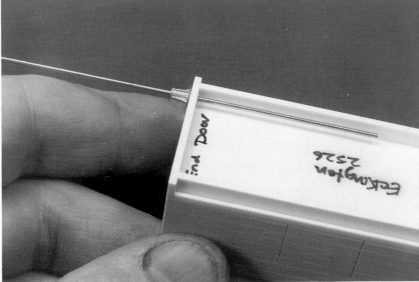

Left: *The finished holes for the buffer.* Right: *Using a 1mm rod to ensure buffer stocks are square in the headstock. The castings are secured with a drop of superglue applied with a pin at the back.*

This picture of a string of wagons being eased over Feltham hump on 21st March 1950, clearly shows the wooden end stanchions. WESSEX COLLECTION

Two views of an ex-Moy wagon in BR days. Note the 'London' top plank. Being lower than the sides, the end door was unusual as this type of end-door hinge would normally have had a full-height door. 14th April 1952.
WESSEX COLLECTION

little spacer to set the stanchions the correct distance apart while fixing them to the ends.

Once they are hardened off, I taper the top part using an emery stick and I find this easier than trying to taper them before fitting them to the model. Alternatively, these could be tapered in a simple filing jig similar to the one used for side-knees on page 107.

Corner plates on full-size wagons were usually 12in wide, although once again this did vary on earlier wagons. These are made from 0.005in styrene sheet (Evergreen 9009).

I use a blunt-edged tool (mine is an old dental tool) to score a fold line 4mm from the edge of the sheet. I do this on a cutting mat but any similarly resilient

An early 7-plank wagon of unknown origin. Note the heavier than usual end stanchions, headstocks extending outside the body, and early type buffers.
ROYE ENGLAND

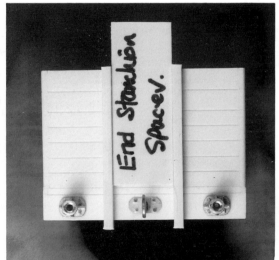
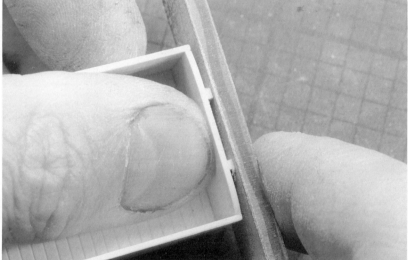

Left: *The spacer used to set end stanchions at the correct distance apart.* Right: *Tapering the tops of the stanchions with an emery stick.*

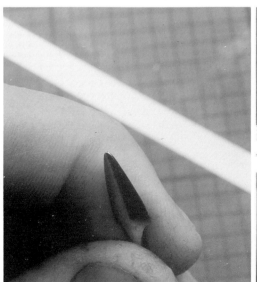
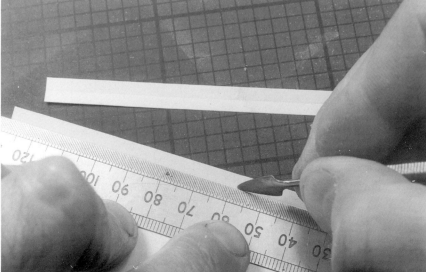

Left: *The tool used to score corner plates.* Right: *The tool in use scoring a line 4mm from the edge of a sheet of 0.005in styrene.*

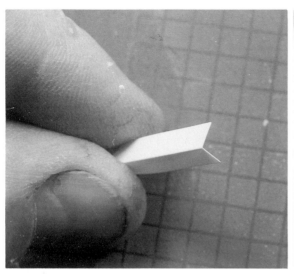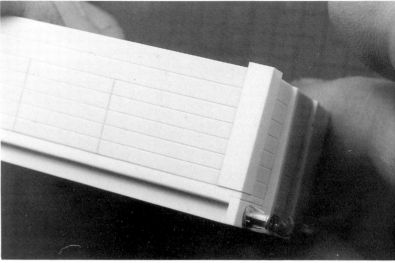

Left: *The plates should bend easily.* Right: *A corner plate fixed in place. The top is trimmed after allowing time to harden.*

This is an Oxcroft wagon of unknown origin. Note the odd planking, Exactoscale W-irons, Masokits brakegear, vees and lever guards. Axleboxes/springs are Ellis type robbed from a Slater's MR wagon kit.

This is an RCH 1923 7-plank wagon. This one has Masokits W-irons, modified ABS brakegear with home-made safety loops, and axlebox/spring castings from MJT Components.

material will do. The idea is to put a fairly deep score in the sheet without cutting through. A strip is cut off the sheet 4mm from this score, thus producing a strip 8mm wide with a deep score down the centre. The corner plates are cut from this strip slightly overlong. If the scoring is done correctly, the corner plates should bend easily between the fingers with a small radius which should fit around the already radiused body corner. These are fixed to the body with a minimum amount of solvent; too much can cause 0.005in styrene to soften and buckle or even adopt the lines of the planking beneath.

RUNNING GEAR

Before finishing the bodywork details, i.e. ironwork, etc., I make up and fit the underframe detail, W-irons and brakegear. I do this partly to avoid the risk of damage through handling the delicate body detail, but also because much of the solebar detail matches up with underframe parts, i.e. crown plates, vee hangers, etc, so it is easier to fit the detail with the running gear in place.

As an example of an early wagon, I have built a model of a conversion from a dumb-buffered vehicle which had been rebuilt with sprung buffers. It is based on a drawing of an Eckington wagon in *Coal Trade Wagons* by L. Tavender, page 20, and a photograph of this wagon appears in *The Wantage Tramway* by N. de Courtais (Wild Swan) page 34.

The construction of these early wagons differed in several details from the more modern types described here.

The original wagon as running on the Wantage Tramway in the 1930s (nearest camera)...

... and here is the finished model.

Side sheeting and ends overlapped the floor, and the side rails fitted between the headstocks. Self-contained buffers were used, presumably because conventional internal buffer springing would not have fitted with the old style underframe construction.

The sides and ends had different planking, so these were scribed separately; this time I made the floor 0.080in less in length as well as width. The sides and ends were assembled around the floor with the underside of the floor flush with the bottom of the sides. The ends had rounded tops. I did this before assembling the body.

End stanchions were fitted next, leaving them overlong, for support while fitting the headstocks, before trimming to length and tapering the top.

I made the side rails from 0.030in x 0.050in strip and used the same solebar material as the other wagons, although I had to reduce the inside of the ends to clear the shanks of the buffers. On reflection, it would have been better to have used 0.040in material in this case.

To represent the self-contained buffers, I modified some whitemetal castings of GWR Churchward-style tapered loco buffers by removing the steps; these were then fitted in the same way as the ABS buffers on pages 19 and 96.

No outside corner plates were fitted to this wagon, only some small angles at the top. The plank ends were exposed, so these were put in with a scalpel.

This wagon had an 8ft 0in wheelbase, so it was a good opportunity to use the Exactoscale separate axleguards. The brake gear was made up from Masokits components, the individual etches for each item making it much easier to use with odd wheelbase lengths.

Exactoscale supply a fold-up assembly jig to set the axleguards to the exact wheelbase dimension. I found this was too wide when folded up and prevented the axleguards being set the correct distance apart, so I snapped off the side pieces and used them separately, which worked perfectly well.

The axleguards were soldered to a piece of 0.010in brass sheet, which fitted between the solebars. The brake gear was

built up on this using the methods described for Masokits brakegear on page 78.

The brake gear was shortened to fit the 8ft 0in wheelbase by simply redrilling the brake shoe hole in the push rods 2mm closer to the centre and cutting off the excess.

Brakes were only fitted to one side of the wagon and there was only one V-hanger fitted inside the solebar, the

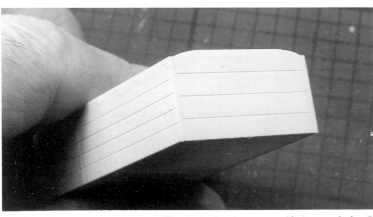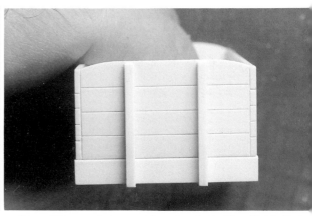

Left: *Ex-dumb-buffered wagon. The body has been assembled around the floor. Note difference between side and end planking.* Right: *End stanchions and headstocks fitted and trimmed to length, also visible ends of planks marked.*

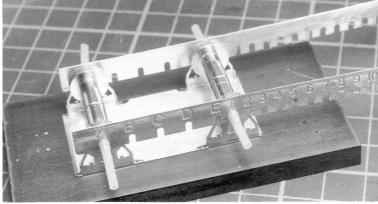

Left: *This shows the ends of the solebars cut away to clear buffer shanks.* Right: *Exactoscale separate axleguards assembled onto a piece of brass using the modified jig.*

Ready to fit to the wagon.

The wagon nearly finished, showing the modified Masokits brakegear. The bottom ears have been removed from the brake shoes. Note the vertical strip supporting the brake rod instead of an outside V-hanger and the wooden door stop.

outside end of the brake shaft being supported by a single vertical strip.

Axleboxes and springs came from a Slater's Charles Roberts underframe kit.

FINAL DETAILING

Most of the final detailing on these wagons consists of the various pieces of ironwork which on real wagons hold them all together. I cut most of these parts using simple tools and jigs which helped to speed up the process.

Much of the solebar detail, crown plates, washer plates and other small pieces of ironwork on the body were stamped out with punches made from silver steel. Ordinary mild steel would do but would not keep its edge so well. I

The inside of the wagon. Note the diagonal ironwork is opposite to normal.

Punches used to produce ironwork detail.

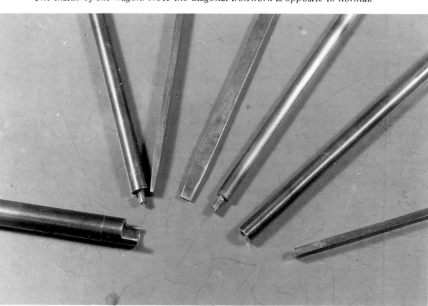

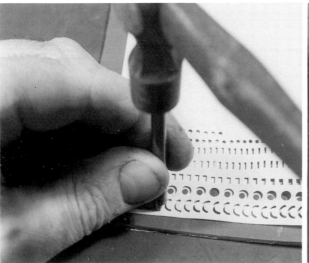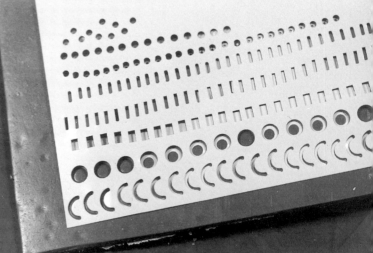

The punch in use. This is best done on a firm surface like the back doorstep.

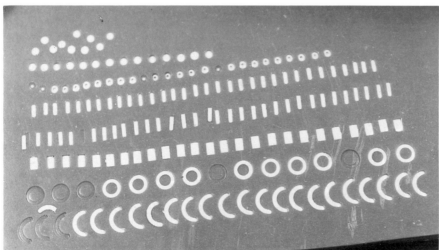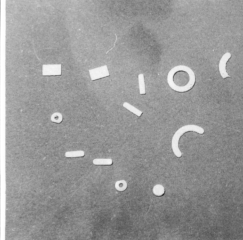

Left: *Here are the results. They are easily removed by bending the plastic or picking them out with a sharp scalpel.* Right: *Here are some of the finished parts.*

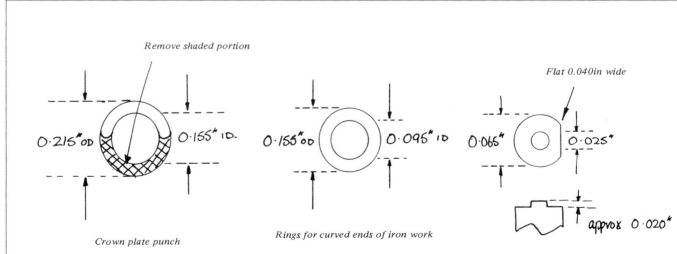

Remove shaded portion

0.215"OD   0.155" ID.

Crown plate punch

0.155"OD   0.095" ID

Rings for curved ends of iron work

Flat 0.040in wide

0.065"   0.025"

approx 0.020"

Punch for door bar ends and end door hinge eyes

have given relevant details of the common ones for those who wish to make them. Whilst most can be simply filed to shape, a lathe makes life easier.

The parts are punched from 0.005in styrene onto a piece of thick plastic sheet; mine is the stuff used for protecting underground cables. I acquired an offcut when our street was being laid with cable TV.

The rest of the ironwork or strapping was cut from 0.005in styrene using another simple cutting jig. I think Chris Crofts described a similar jig in *Model Railway Journal* No. 15. I only used this for producing 0.005in thickness strips. Most of the other sizes are available from the Evergreen range.

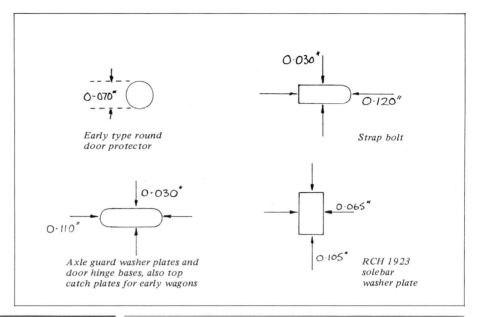

Early type round door protector

Strap bolt

Axle guard washer plates and door hinge bases, also top catch plates for early wagons

RCH 1923 solebar washer plate

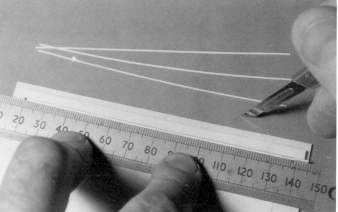

Left: *The jig for cutting 0.030in wide strips used to represent ironwork. The main part is a sheet of 0.040in styrene approximately 6in x 4in with a 4mm wide strip of 0.040in stuck along one edge. A small piece of 0.030in (or whatever width strip is required) is fixed at each end to set the width of the strips being cut.* Right: *The 0.005in sheet is pushed against the edge strip and the rule against the 0.030in pieces...*

... and with a sharp scalpel, strips are cut off.

When fitting small details such as this, a support for the model makes life much easier. There is nothing worse than trying to fit small items with the wagon wobbling all over the place. My support is cheaply made from ¼in Obechi and lined with foam with a few odd pieces to hold the model firmly.

The picture should explain all; just make it to suit your requirements. Mine is large enough to accept vans as well.

I usually fit the internal ironwork first, as most of this can be done without any risk of damaging outside detail.

Side and end knees
On full-sized wagons, these were heavy L-shaped brackets, the bottom section being hidden below the floor boards. On the model, it is only necessary to represent the vertical tapered section. These are fitted each side of the drop door and at the door end of the wagon. I use 0.030in x 0.040in (Evergreen 122) and file the taper in a simple jig. This is made from a strip of 0.040in styrene, 20mm wide and about 6in long. Two pieces about 20mm long were cut from this and fixed to the remaining strip with a 0.040in slot between them. In the bottom of this slot I fitted a wedge-shaped piece of strip to produce a tapered slot

Support for working on the model.

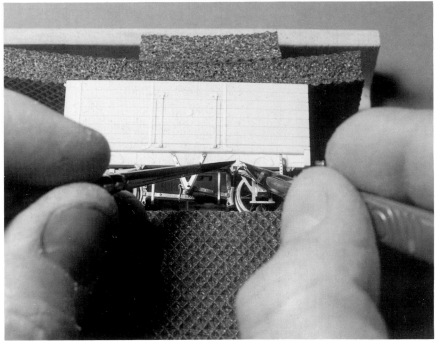

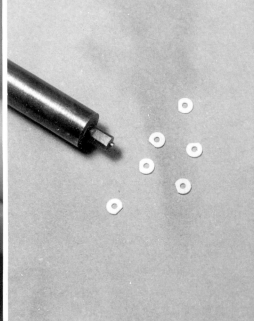

Left: *The foam sheet came from an old camping mat.* Right: *End door bar eyes punched from 0.005in sheet.*

0.020in deep at one end and 0.030in deep at the other.

The top of the knees at the door end usually incorporated an eye to support the end of the hinge bar. On the RCH 1923 types, this ironwork was sometimes extended diagonally inside the wagon, whilst the outside diagonal had a similar eye at the top for additional support. I make these eyes using a punch, as described for the ironwork details. They should be 0.010in thick, but I find it difficult to get a clean cut using thicker sheet, so I laminate two 0.005in pieces.

Before fitting the end knees, I drill the holes in the body 0.7mm for the hinge bar; another little jig makes this

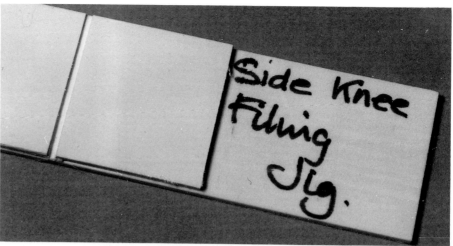

This is the jig for filing side knees, showing the tapered slot.

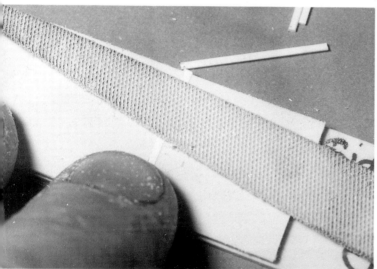

Left: *The jig in use. A fairly coarse flat file is best for these jobs.* Right: *And here is the result.*

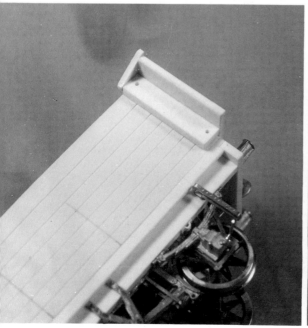

Left and right: *Drilling jig for end-door bar hinge.*

A wagon interior which shows the details being modelled opposite. The thickness of the side knees are evident and this picture also shows the eyes at the top of the end knees which supported the end-door hinge bar. The poor condition of this wagon illustrates the typical battered state of the interior.

Here is the outside of the same wagon showing the eye at the top of the diagonal which supported the end of the hinge bar with a retaining nut at each end.

easier and saves marking out the hole positions. It was made to be used both on the right and left side of the wagon. The hinge bars are from 0.025in rod (Evergreen 219). I cut them a bit overlong to allow trimming back after fitting the outside eyes and nuts. The rod is pushed through one hole and four eyes threaded on before pushing through the other side. The rod is fixed with solvent, making sure the pair of eyes each side have the flats at the bottom. Two more eyes are fitted each side to represent the outside end of the vertical or diagonal ironwork, depending on the wagon being modelled.

The knees are fitted next, the end ones being shortened to butt up against the end door bar eyes.

End-door bar fitted. The eyes have been fitted to represent the tops of the RCH 1923 type end knees.

Left: *This shows the outside of the same wagon. Two more eyes are fitted here to represent the ends of the diagonal ironwork.* Right: *An RCH 1923 8-plank wagon, with side and end knees fitted.*

Left: *RCH 1923 7-plank wagon showing internal door bands fitted with top sections of hinges. Nuts have also been fitted to ends of bar.* Right: *Gloucester 7-plank wagon with internal diagonals and small corner plates fitted.*

This excellent picture, taken on 17th April 1940, is full of interest. The door retainer bar of the wagon in the foreground is as described here, clearly showing how the vertical ironwork wrapped over the bar. The hinge bar on this wagon can be seen running through the eyes at the top of the end knees with a cotter on the right to retain it. The door was hung on three extension loops of the internal ironwork. Note the odd buffers, one without the floor-retaining lug, also the two straps bolted to the headstock which also retained the floor. The loaded wagon on the left shows a similar hinge bar, this time with the bar going through the top plank into an eye on the outside diagonal ironwork with nuts to retain it.

NATIONAL RAILWAY MUSEUM

End door bars

I make these from 0.010in x 0.040in strip (Evergreen 102). The eyes at each end are made from the same punchings used for the end door hinge eyes, and these are laminated as before and fixed in place at the ends of the bar. When these were hard, I drilled through into the ends of the sides and fitted stubs of 0.025in rod to represent the retaining cotters.

The vertical bands on the doors of real wagons were joggled to wrap over the door bar. To represent this, the vertical sections are fitted first to butt up against the bar and then short pieces are fitted to overlap the bar slightly. Finally, little slivers of 0.005in are tucked into the gaps at the ends of these.

Gloucester 7-plank wagon with end door bar and eyes fitted. 0.6mm holes were drilled into the side planking to accept cotters.

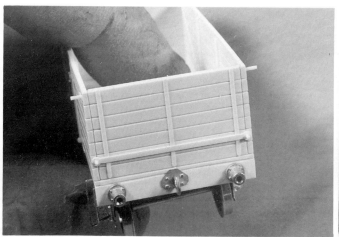

Left: *Gloucester 7-plank wagon with cotters and door bands fitted.* Right: *RCH 1923 7-plank wagon with door bands finished, and detail over the bar as described in the text. Note the buffers and hook plates overlap the floor end. This was to retain the floor when end tipping. It has ABS buffers and Ambis hook and plate.*

Here is an RCH wagon with a similar end-door bar, buffers and hook plate to the model above.
WESSEX COLLECTION

Two RCH 1923 wagons in very poor condition, clearly showing the typical condition of these vehicles at the end of their lives. The wagon in the top picture appears to have been repaired with a thinner plank, third from the top, requiring some packing under the top door catches. Note also the patch to the left of the door and the rotten side rail. The left-hand W-iron looks a bit out of true, probably through weakening of the underframe. It would be quite a challenge to model a wagon in this state.

Left: *Gloucester 6-plank wagon fitted with bottom hinge plates, verticals and early-type rounded catch plates.* Centre: *RCH 1923 8-plank wagon with rectangular catch plates.* Right: *RCH 1923 8-plank wagon with bottoms of door hinges fitted and 0.010in top catches overlapping vertical door bands.*

Left: *This picture clearly shows how the vertical door bands overlapped the door.* Right: *RCH 1923 7-plank wagon with 0.005in pieces added to overlap catches slightly. Gaps at the sides are filled with slivers of 0.010in.*

CTY. P. MILLARD

Side door hinges and catches

Bottom hinge plates on the side rails are punchings, as described earlier. These can also be used for the top door catch plates if appropriate. Earlier wagons often had rounded ends to these plates (check prototype); later wagons had square-ended plates, and these are cut from 0.005in x 0.030in strip.

The bottom of the hinge, which in the real thing is actually the end of the hinge bar rolled round, is represented with a short length of 0.035in rod (Evergreen 220) filed half round and cut into 0.030in lengths. These are fixed to the centre of the bottom plates.

The vertical part of the hinge is made from 0.010in x 0.030in strip overlapping the top of the door slightly.

Door catches

Here I copied the methods described by Chris Crofts in *Model Railway Journal* No. 14. The photographs and sketches should make this clear.

The Chris Crofts method of making door catches.

1.

2.

3.

1. Baseplate from 0.005in x 0.030in.
2. Add catch from 0.010in x 0.030in.
3. Add piece of 0.005in.
4. Insert slivers of 0.010in at sides.
5. Side view of catch.

4.   5.

RCH 1923 7-plank wagon. Slivers of 0.010in are added to the top and bottom of catches to finish them off.

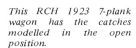

This RCH 1923 7-plank wagon has the catches modelled in the open position.

An RCH 1923 7-plank wagon with coke raves is seen here partially unloaded.

ROYE ENGLAND

Early pattern door catches

Earlier wagons used a hasp and staple type of door catch with loose cotter-type door retainers. I make these from 0.010in x 0.040in strip (the photos explain this). The only tricky part is rounding the ends of the catches. I could have made a punch for these, but instead I cut off a supply of strips about 5mm long, and, holding a few in a pair of stout tweezers, round the ends with a fine emery stick. These are cut to length and fixed in place. When hard, a 0.5mm hole is drilled to accept a stub of 0.020in rod (Evergreen 218) to represent the cotter.

It was quite common for the side knee washer plates adjacent to the side doors to have curved ends to align with the ends of the diagonal ironwork. I make the

Gloucester 6-plank wagon showing the earlier style door catches.

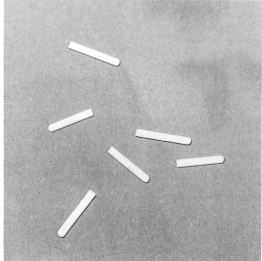

Left: *Shaping the ends of a batch of door catches using a fine emery stick . . .* Right: *. . . and the result.*

Here is an old 5-plank wagon with the early type door catches. Note the curved bottoms of the vertical ironwork each side of the door. The diagonal ironwork was inside the body. Note also the wooden door stops.
CTY. P. MILLARD

Two private owner wagons with cupboard style doors. This was a common feature of Scottish wagons.
ROYE ENGLAND

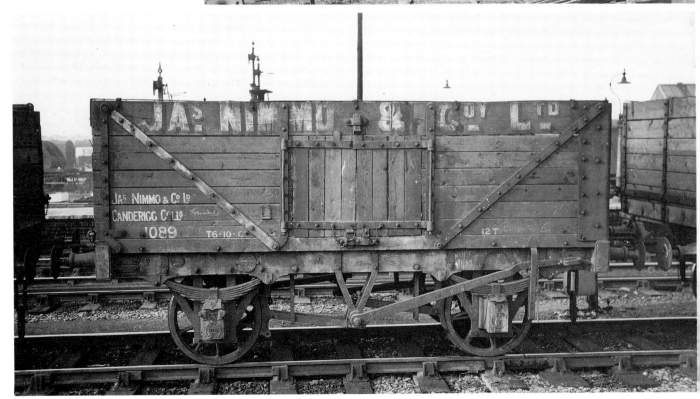

curved sections from small pieces cut from rings punched out of 0.005in.

The diagonal ironwork usually had a joggle where it crossed over corner plates. To represent this, I fix the main part to the wagon sides, then with the back of a scalpel blade, put a crease against the corner plate. This is left to harden, then the rest is pressed down and secured with a spot of solvent.

Left: *Using sections cut from punched rings to make the curved ends of side knee washer plates.* Right: *This is how they are used.*

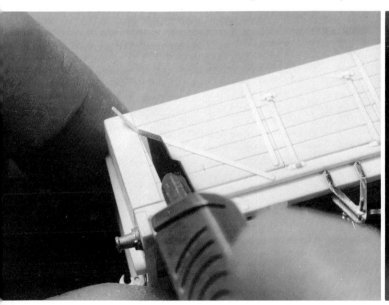

Left: *Using the back of a scalpel blade to form a joggle in the diagonal ironwork where it fits over the corner plates.* Right: *The loose end is then stuck down with a touch of solvent.*

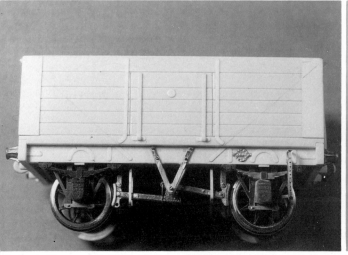

Left: *A Gloucester 6-plank side-door wagon. Springs and axleboxes are Slater's, V-hangers and W-irons are Masokits, and the rest of the solebar detail is punched from 0.005in styrene. Brakegear is modified ABS. Note one brake shoe has the bottom lug removed.* Right: *Another Gloucester wagon, this time a 7-plank end-door version. This wagon has D&S rocking W-irons, MJT Gloucester axleboxes, and modified 9-leaf springs to represent 7-leaf type, modified ABS brakes and Masokits vees and registration plates.*

Three pictures which show some variations of iron-work. This one shows the diagonals overlapping the side knee washer plates.
CTY. P. MILLARD

A wagon with curved bottoms to the side knee washer plates. Note the raised end and the label clip on the second plank.
CTY. P. MILLARD

Left: *A closer view of capping strips.* Right: *The label clip being used on an ex-PO slope-sided steel mineral.*

Capping strips and retaining clips, where appropriate, are made as described in the section on Cambrian kits (page 27).

Label clips

I make these from the waste material after punching out the strap bolt detail. They need to be cut as close to the hole as possible. They are fixed in place with a tiny drop of solvent, and a sliver of 0.010in fitted at the bottom represents the spring. The position of label clips varied a lot; sometimes they were on the solebars and sometimes on the body sides.

Horse hooks and grab irons

I use 0.008in phosphor-bronze wire (Eileen's) for very fine handles, etc. I find this better as it is much stiffer than brass or nickel wire. I make drills from 0.010in steel guitar string for these jobs. They are perfectly satisfactory for drilling small holes in plastic, and conventional drills in these small sizes are very expensive and break too easily.

To make the drill, a short length of the string is held in a pin chuck with about 4mm protruding. The business end is shaped to a flat point with an oilstone.

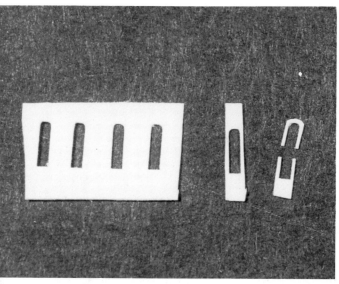 

Left: Label clips cut from waste material after punching strap bolts. Right: The clip in position on the wagon. All the solebar detail is made from 0.005in punchings.

An RCH 1923 wagon, photographed at Kettering on 16th September 1952, showing the normal position of horse hook and label clips on the solebar. Shown in BR condition but with the pre-war livery still clearly visible, these wagons were uprated from 12 tons to 13 tons capacity during the war. Note also the open spoke wheels. The photographer noted the colour as grey with white lettering, but this was probably faded from black.

WESSEX COLLECTION

I have not found the shape too critical so long as there is a point of sorts. Used in a pin chuck with gentle pressure, they soon go through styrene. The hooks and handles are secured with a spot of super-glue.

Suggested shape for piano wire drills. The actual shape is not too critical so long as a point is formed. Twiddled in a pin vice, they quickly drill through styrene.

A Gloucester 5-plank wagon showing the end grab handles, gap filler below the side door, and central wooden door stop. L. E. COPELAND

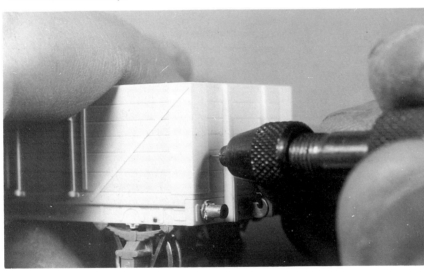

Left: *Drilling holes for grab handles using a home-made drill.*

Left: *Grab handles are secured with a spot of superglue on the inside. When it has cured, the ends of the wire are trimmed off with a scalpel.*
Right: *The finished model, another Eckington wagon, this time a 6-plank. Note the odd plank widths, and end grab irons. The Ellis pattern axleboxes and springs came from a Slater's Midland underframe.*

Horse hook fitted to the solebar of a 6-plank wagon. Note the patch over the bottom of the corner plate; this was to repair a rusted area.

The wagons illustrated here show the different positions of horse hooks and label clips. A. ATTEWELL

Another Scottish cupboard-door wagon with small wartime lettering, photographed at Kettering on 16th September 1952. Note the early single-shoe brakes.
WESSEX COLLECTION

Bearing spring stops

These are a distinctive feature and are tricky things to make from scratch. Some were solid castings, others were steel pressings. The solid type are easy to fabricate from styrene, but I felt the pressed steel type would be easier to produce with another simple tool using the boiling water method.

The tool is soldered up from brass scraps. The main parts are approximately ½in wide by about 3in long, the thickness is not important; I used some scrap etching about 0.020in thick. One piece has two short lengths of 0.020in brass soldered flush with one end, with a 1mm gap between them, whilst the other has a piece of 0.5mm square brass wire soldered in the centre of its end to correspond with the gap left between the two lengths on the opposite leg. The two legs are soldered together at the other end to make a tweezer-like tool. The only important point is to ensure the 0.5mm square wire falls in the centre of the 1mm wide slot. The photos explain this.

A short piece of 0.010in x 0.040in styrene is held in the end of the tool and gripped with tweezers while it is held in near-boiling water for a second or two, then cooled in cold water. A batch of spring stops can be made very quickly and is a lot less tedious than making them from scratch.

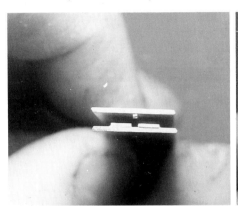

Left: *The business end of the spring stop tool. The 0.5mm wire on the top piece must be central between the other two pieces at the bottom.*
Right: *The other end is soldered together with a piece of scrap etch between to keep the main parts parallel.*

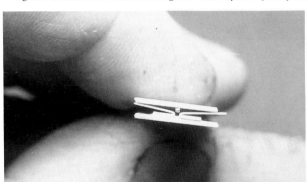
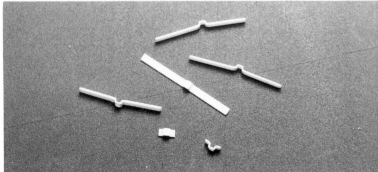

Left: *This shows the tool with a piece of 0.010in strip after forming.* Right: *Spring stops produced with the tool . . .*

. . . and fitted to a wagon.

This wagon was copied from a photograph in Private Owner Wagons Vol. 3 by Bill Hudson, and shows a wagon overhauled in 1940 with full livery.

Another Oxcroft wagon, a 1923 RCH design renumbered with a 'P' prefix by British Railways and still in pretty fair condition when photographed in the early 1950s.
ROYE ENGLAND

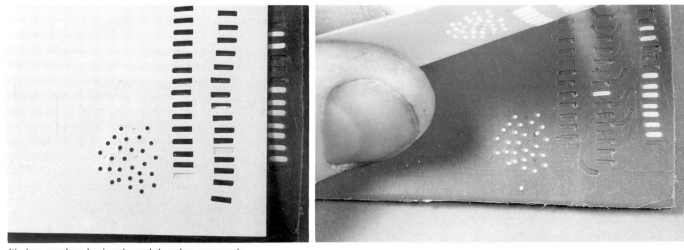

Washers produced using the end door bar eye punch.

Bolt head detail

The bolt head detail must now be represented and this can only be effectively done by applying individual 'nuts' cut from 0.010in square styrene. Wooden-bodied wagons were held together with round-headed coach bolts which were usually pushed through from inside the body, with square nuts outside. The nuts on the solebars usually had individual washer plates or separate washers in the case of 1923 wagons. I thought it would be nice to represent these washers, which might seem a bit over the top, but for those who wish to bother with the washers, here is how I do it.

Washers fitted along the siderail and solebars of a 1923 RCH 7-plank wagon. Note also the capping strips and clips fitted.

This picture clearly shows the washers under the nuts on the side rail and solebars on a 6-plank wagon. Note the 9-leaf springs and Ellis axleboxes. The body was painted but, unusually, the side rails and underframe were bare wood.
CTY. P. MILLARD

I noticed when punching out the end door bar eyes that the little dots left behind after punching out the rings, might make good washers. This time the punch is only tapped very lightly to punch out just the middle dot. Too much pressure and they become too deeply embedded in the plastic sheet. I could have made a new punch from larger diameter rod but the original is fine if used carefully.

The actual 'nuts' are cut from 0.010in wide strips of 0.010in styrene. I usually cut plenty of strips as inevitably they will vary slightly. I then sort out which look the same width and use them as a batch, otherwise the 'nuts' will look odd if they vary in size. The selected strips are cut into approximately 50mm lengths and stuck with Mek-pak to a piece of Paxolin or any smooth material which is not

Here is the set-up I use when applying nuts to a wagon. Note the short brush handle – a long-handled brush gets in the way. I kept poking it in my eye.

Left: The 0.010in strip of 'nut' material fixed to a piece of Paxolin with a supply of nuts ready cut. Right: Applying the nuts to a wagon.

affected by solvent (a piece of Formica laminate would do). Then let this harden thoroughly.

Using a new 10A or 15A scalpel blade, I cut off a supply of cubes as accurately as possible, rejecting any odd-shaped ones. Having the strips fixed to the Paxolin makes it easier than trying to hold this fine strip.

The 'nuts' are picked up with the point of the blade and positioned on the model with a spot of solvent. When I have finished a wagon side, I go over all the nuts with a loaded brush, using just enough to leave a tiny puddle of solvent around each nut. This is left to dry thoroughly (overnight is best) before giving the wagon side a brisk brushing over with a soft fibreglass brush, one with

A finished side of an RCH 1923 7-plank wagon. The washers do show! I have also fitted the solebar to siderail brackets.

Left: *Fibreglass brushes with fairly long bristles, approximately 6 mm. I find these less harsh on plastic than short stubby ones.* Right: *Giving the finished side a good brush over. This will reveal any loose nuts.*

Another ex-Scottish wagon with an odd plank arrangement and 3-plank door. Note the lifting catch type end door retainers instead of the more common pin and cotter arrangement.

COLLECTION R. J. ESSERY

This view clearly shows the bottom door catch to the left of the V-hanger and the chain fitted to the safety pin which locked the door catch closed.
CTY. P. MILLARD

about 6mm of bristle showing. This removes the glaze left by the solvent and reveals any loose nuts. If all is well, do another side. I usually have a few wagons on the go, so I can chop and change amongst them while waiting for one to dry.

Two types of bottom door catch. This one is the type modelled . . .

Bottom door catches
To represent these, I drill a 0.4mm hole into the base of the solebar just below the left-hand edge of the side door, and insert a piece of 0.4mm brass wire. This is cut to leave approximately 2.5mm projecting from the bottom of the solebar, and is then bent inwards slightly. Each side of this I fix a square of 0.010in x 0.040in strip, followed by some tiny triangular pieces each side of the pin to represent the vertical parts of the catch.

. . . and this type has an enclosed pivot for the handle.

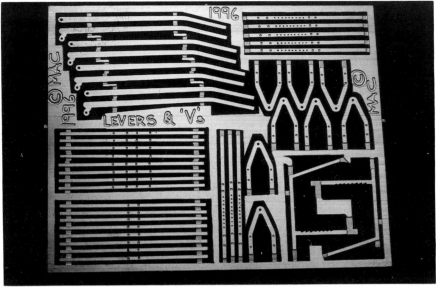

Brake levers and side door springs

Brake levers are from the Masokits levers and vees fret. These are bent to shape, ensuring they fit into the recess at the top of the lever guard, and then I just solder them to the brake shaft. They could be fixed to the guard but I haven't found this necessary.

Masokits also make door springs, but I prefer to make some more authentic-looking ones myself from 0.012in x 0.050in wide brass from some etch scrap. I drill two 0.4mm holes about 2mm apart, close to one end, and cut off a piece slightly overlong.

This is bent to shape, then trimmed to length before being fixed to the solebars with a spot of superglue. When this has cured, I drill into the solebar and glue

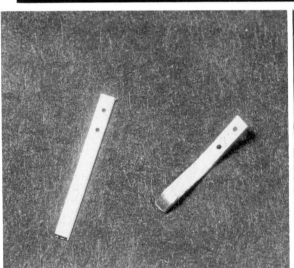

Left: *Home-made door springs.* Right: *Here is the door protector fixed in place with a spot of superglue. The bottom door catch can be seen to the left of the V-hanger.*

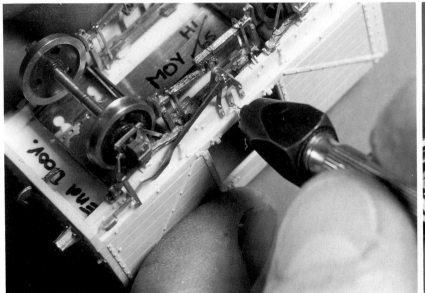

Left: *Drilling holes to accept 0.4mm wire pins.* Right: *Pins fitted with a spot of superglue. These are trimmed off to leave a little stub showing.*

in stubs of 0.4mm wire. These are then trimmed off to represent bolts.

Chains

Finally, I fit some 'chains' to the end doors. The chain is represented by very fine copper wire twisted together, then fitted to the end doors by gluing into 0.3mm drilled holes.

This shows the chains fitted to an end-door wagon.

Left: Side door cotter chains made from fine copper wire and glued into small holes. Right: A Gloucester 6-plank wagon lettered with transfers from Dragon Models.

A finished scratchbuilt 1923 RCH 8-plank wagon lettered with POWsides transfers.

Another scene in Gloucester Carriage & Wagon Co's workshop, showing 1923 RCH 7-plank wagons being painted. The combination of what appears to be a grey colour and the fitting of end door handles could indicate that these were built for the LMS. This picture also shows the side and end door fastenings very clearly.

PAINTING, LETTERING AND WEATHERING

Before the models are painted, I use a chemical blackening solution on the etched parts. I don't think it is a good idea just to paint the underframe as this can clog up the springing. By blackening it first, it is only necessary to virtually weather the underframe with a dry brush technique.

I decant a supply of blackening solution into a plastic dish and liberally apply it to the metal parts. It doesn't matter if the coverage is not perfect. Rinse off the solution in clean water and dry thoroughly.

I painted the scratchbuilt wagons with acrylic car paint applied direct from an aerosol. Red primer makes a good match for red oxide. These models were all quite heavily weathered, so getting the base colours spot on is not important. I also used grey primer for BR grey. The other models described in this book were all painted with colours from the Phoenix Precision range; these are best applied with an airbrush. It is not necessary to prime the plastic before painting but it is best to degrease with lighter fuel to remove finger marks, etc. I masked off

the underframe roughly below the solebar using wide masking tape from a DIY store. This is just to keep most of the paint away from the underframe and suspension parts. The tape also makes a useful holding device.

When using an aerosol, try it first on a piece of scrap material to judge the spraying distance as they do vary. I really prefer an airbrush as they are so much more controllable, but with care very good results can be achieved using aerosols.

Left: *Applying chemical blackening. Using a fairly stiff brush and agitating the solution works best.* Right: *Here is the result. It doesn't matter if the coverage is not 100%.*

Acrylic colours used on these models.

Spraying a model with an aerosol. Note the masking tape doubling as a hand hold.

LETTERING TRADITIONAL PRIVATE OWNER WAGONS

 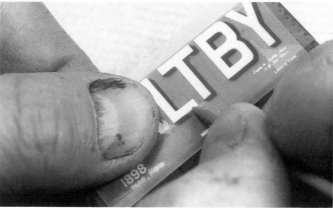

Left: POWsides lettering positioned on wagon and held at each end with Magic tape. Right: Rubbing down the lettering using a plastic knitting needle. Make sure all the lettering is detached from the film.

This shows how the lettering looks after removal of the backing film. It is not pressed tightly around raised detail.

Using a piece of thick rubber band under a scalpel handle to press the lettering well into the detail.

Whatever paint I use, I allow at least 24 hours before applying transfers.

The aerosol paints are not dead flat but have a slight sheen. This is an advantage as the surface takes transfers and dry print lettering more easily. The Precision paints are dead flat so I burnish the areas where the transfers are to be placed with a cotton bud.

The lettering on the private owner wagons described here comes from the POWsides and Dragon Models ranges. The instructions with these suggest applying these before assembly of the model. However, I don't find this practical, especially with scratchbuilt models, and, in any case, I prefer to paint the complete model first. I have not found any difficulty applying transfers to finished wagons.

First cut the transfer and backing sheet about 6mm less than the length of the wagon side, taking care not to touch the sticky side as it is quite delicate. I fix a piece of Scotch magic tape about 25mm long to each end of the transfer which is then carefully positioned on the wagon side, the sticky tape being pulled tightly around the ends of the wagon to hold the transfer firmly.

I use a blunt pointed device (a plastic knitting needle is ideal) to rub the lettering down firmly all over the wagon, pressing it around the raised detail and ensuring that it is all detached from the carrier film. Support the wagon side with a finger and thumb.

Now carefully remove the film; some of the adhesive from the magic tape may remain on the model, but this is easily removed with a cotton bud moistened with white spirit. However, be careful not to get any on the lettering.

At this stage the lettering will not have gone tightly around the raised detail. I have found a piece of thick rubber band pressed down firmly with the end of a scalpel handle or something similar is very effective for this. This may cause some of the lettering to crack a little around details, but it is easily touched in with a spot of paint if you want a perfect job. However, as most wagons soon lost their newness after a short time in service, I don't consider this a problem and prefer to let the weathering hide any blemishes.

At this stage the lettering is quite vulnerable and needs protecting with a coat of varnish. POWsides recommend Letracoat or Frisk but I have used Humbrol or Ronseal Matt, and both have proved totally satisfactory. Apply this very sparingly just over the lettering so that it dries very quickly. A thick coat can cause the edges of the lettering to lift. I leave this to dry thoroughly overnight, then apply a second coat thinned with about 30% pure turpentine, as this is much cheaper than enamel thinners and smells nice too. It is important to seal the lettering well, especially if the model is to be weathered.

After pressing down the lettering with a rubber band.

A final protective coat of varnish.

The finished Maltby wagon. This has been only lightly weathered to represent a wagon in fairly new condition.

Here is another MOT wagon, on the coaling plant at Kentish Town motive power depot on 23rd November 1947. This became BR Diagram 1/102 which was an all-welded version of Diagram 1/105. Note the different pattern pressed steel door and back-to-front solebar with the channel facing inwards.

R. F. ROBERTS

LETTERING BR WAGONS AND STEEL MINERALS

On BR standard unfitted wagons, the insignia was applied to black patches. These can be painted on by hand, but, as they varied in size to suit the numbers, I have found it easier to make up the numbers, tare weights, etc, onto plain black transfer film using Methfix transfers from HMRS (for BR wagons, use sheets 25 and 26). I purchased my black film from Fourtrack Models of Harrow; it is also available from model aircraft suppliers sold as decal film. I make up the required insignia, then varnish over them. After the varnish has dried, they can be cut to shape and fitted to the model.

The two MOT liveried wagons were painted with Phoenix Precision LMS bauxite. When this was hard, the areas where lettering was to be applied was burnished, as mentioned before, with a cotton bud to smooth the surface. No commercial transfers are available for this particular insignia.

I made up the lettering from Methfix sheet No. 12 (LNER wagons) for the letters 'M.O.T.' and numbers from sheet No. 6 (LMS wagons). The end door stripe and bottom door markings are on sheet 26 (BR pre TOPS insignia).

Once again this was all protected with a thin coat of matt varnish.

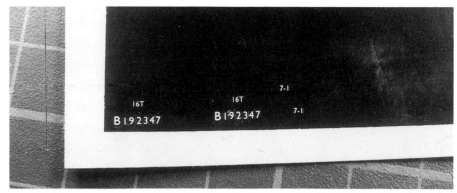

Making up BR wagon numbering on black transfer film.

These are cut to size and fitted to the wagon.

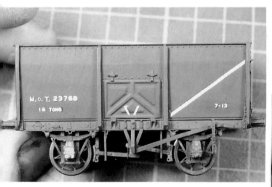

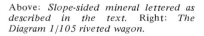

Above: *Slope-sided mineral lettered as described in the text.* Right: *The Diagram 1/105 riveted wagon.*

HAND LETTERING

by PAUL KARAU

produced really beautiful characters in ways which we would never predict.

It can be quite exciting once you've managed two or three of the letters, and even if they aren't perfect but convey the character of the original, you should feel encouraged to persist. Minor mistakes can be adjusted by scraping with a sharpened matchstick or a gentle touch with a Swann-Morton No. 10 scalpel blade held between thumb and forefinger, whilst more serious errors can be corrected using a small stiff brush just moistened with turps or white spirit.

I did all the shading with Humbrol matt black paint, the application of which can tidy up (or ruin!) the edges of the lettering. Again the shading can be refined with the gentle touch of a scalpel blade.

I think it's really all down to strict observation of the photo you are copying. As you can see, I am no expert, but with concentrated effort I managed to produce a result which looks OK — to me anyway — and in any case weathering can hide a multitude of sins.

Rather than add turpentine to a large quantity of matt white, I prefer to mix them together in a small puddle in the bottom of a glass jar, the sides and rim of which I wipe the brush on after each charge. That way I can easily adjust the mix according to feel and, for that matter, compensate for the way the paint thickens during a lettering session.

You don't need to be a signwriter to letter wagons by hand, but you do need to be observant and have at least some patience. The plank lines are a wonderful guide and assuming that the model matches the picture you are working from, the ironwork is a great help in establishing the positions of various letters which, of course, helps with the overall letter spacing.

I use Humbrol matt white No. 34 thinned with turpentine and applied with the best quality brush I can find. The one I favour most is a Winsor & Newton Series 12, No. 000, which I treasure. I have since bought at least three more from various art shops but they are nowhere near as good as the one I use most, so my advice is to be choosy.

Sitting comfortably at a desk or table with a good desk lamp is essential and if you can't be bothered to make up a cradle like the one shown, then two or three books of the right thickness to bring your hand level with the top of the wagon will suffice.

I begin by lightly sketching the position of the letters on the side of the wagon with thin strokes which can be broadened later. Don't worry if you aren't happy with the position of anything because it is easy to wash off the offending lines with another paintbrush loaded with turps or white spirit.

Rather than worry too much about the shape of each letter at this stage, it may be easier to crudely mark just the verticals and horizontals, whilst for less straightforward letters, like a 'P' or an 'S', try marking just the tops or leading edges of the curves to see how it all works out. When you are satisfied with the overall spacing, you can start to fill out each character, broadening the lines on whichever side further improves the spacing or helps to capture the character of the letter.

The key to the final appearance is following the shape of each letter as closely as possible, with total disregard for your own style of handwriting. You will often find the signwriter

This photo shows how the roughly sketched-in spidery lettering is broadened to the proper width. The edges can be sharpened up with a scalpel blade which can also be used to shape up any of the smaller lettering or even to create the hole in a letter 'O' or 'A' if they've filled in or gone out of shape. The tiny lettering is a series of meaningless strokes — just an illusion.

The completed paint job.

Model and prototype pictures of some Sheepbridge wagons. The top picture shows the wagon as originally lettered with POWsides transfers. It was obvious that the lettering shapes were not very good, particularly the letters 'P', 'B', 'D' and 'G'. These were modified by scraping with a scalpel and retouching with brushed enamels to produce the result here, which looks much more convincing. The number was also altered because the model didn't match the photo of the real 6091 which appears in one of the volumes of Bill Hudson's *Private Owner Wagons*.

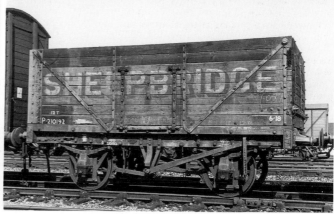

Four examples of Sheepbridge wagons which were painted red oxide with white lettering and black shading. The top views are undated but show pre-war liveries whilst the bottom views were taken on 6th September 1953 and 26th November 1964 respectively. P210192 was built by the Eastwood Wagon Co as part of a batch numbered 201-275 and registered by the LMS in February 1939.

R. J. ESSERY, COLLECTION R. S. CARPENTER and WESSEX COLLECTION

An 8-plank wagon in as-new condition. Note the single grab handle on the end door. The livery was red oxide with white lettering and black shading. The white wheel rims and buffers were for photographic purposes. It is unlikely that wagons would have generally been built like this.
                                                                                                                LENS OF SUTTON

Another Hickleton wagon with the wartime addition of the owner's name in small lettering on the left-hand side. This picture was taken at Cambridge on 29th August 1952.
                                                                                                                WESSEX COLLECTION

Once the lettering is finished, the rest of the painting can be done, i.e. the inside of the wagons, ironwork and underframes. I use Humbrol matt enamels thinned with a little pure turpentine. After thoroughly mixing the paint, a little is decanted into an artists ceramic palette, one with several partitions. These are excellent for this sort of work, especially weathering, as two or three colours plus a drop of thinners can be used together.

WEATHERING

The techniques used for weathering follow the methods described by Martyn Welch in his superb book *The Art of Weathering* (Wild Swan) and I can strongly recommend this to modellers wishing to create lifelike models. For the wagons described here, the following colours are used: Humbrol matt black 33, matt orange 82, matt light brown 62, and grey 64.

I decant a little of each colour into each section of the palette and some pure turpentine into another. I make a thin

The set-up for painting showing palette used for paints.

Left: *This is the ex-dumb-buffered wagon ready for lettering.* Right: *The inside of a wagon painted to represent unpainted woodwork using a mixture of Humbrol light brown 62 and grey 64. The ironwork has been picked out in black.*

Using a 00 sable brush to paint a corner plate, with Humbrol matt black No. 33.

This is the set-up for a weathering session.

Some of the brushes used for weathering.

wash of black, brown and grey, which is sloshed liberally over the underframe and wheels, and allowed to dry partially. Then, with a stubby brush, I just scrub around all the detail, and, as the thinners dries, an even coat of rusty-looking colour will spread over the underframe, leaving stronger colour in the nooks and crannies.

Let this dry overnight, then using individual colours, various parts are given a dry brushing, i.e. brakes and wheels, to achieve the desired result. This is easier to do than describe. I find it best to keep the paint quite thin and slowly build up the textures required.

The same techniques are used for body work. Until the war, wagons were usually kept in reasonable repair, the liveries were easily visible, and timber work was kept in pretty good condition. During the wartime, when the PO wagon fleet was pooled, the original liveries soon became neglected, and, to identify ownership, the names were painted in small white lettering at the bottom left-hand corners, the intention being to revert to private ownership after the war. In the event, this did not happen and these wagons passed into British Railways ownership without having been painted and only patch repaired for many years. This situation remained until the demise of these wooden wagons in the late '50s/early '60s.

Upon nationalisation, the ex private owner wagon fleet was given a 'P' prefix to the wagon number and these were usually applied to a black patch, although some were applied direct to the wagon side.

Stages in weathering a Cambrian RCH 1923 7-plank to BR condition. After weathering, some of the paint is scraped off a few planks to represent replacements, using a scalpel.

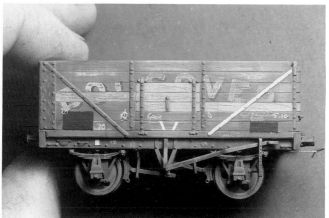

Left: *The planks are then painted to look like bare wood, then weathered down a little and black patches painted on for the numbering.*
Right: *This is how it looked at first, but the result still didn't look quite convincing, so a bit more paintwork was removed*

This is the result, showing a wagon getting towards the end of its life.

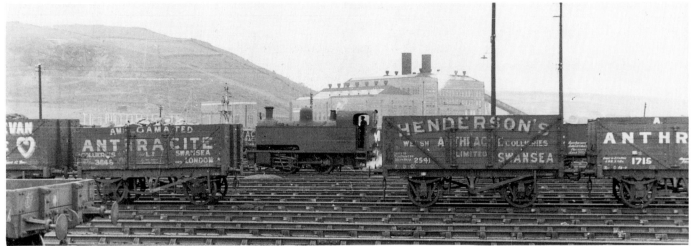

A few private owner wagons on their home territory, shown here at Danygraig, Swansea, on 17th August 1935.
    H. F. WHEELLER

A Stephenson Clarke wagon with a steel underframe. This was the final development of the 1923 RCH design. The livery was grey with white lettering shaded black, and Indian red corner plates. These pictures were taken at Cardington on 7th October 1939.
    WESSEX COLLECTION

A selection of wagons in postwar condition. The identity of the Stanton Massey wagon would have been lost with the replacement of planks were it not for the small lettering.

CTY. P. MILLARD

The postwar scene, dilapidated private owner wagons reliably continuing in service with ever-decreasing evidence of their pre-war liveries. The grass-grown sidings in this picture of Lydney in 1946 echo the neglect of a hard-pressed railway system.

L. E. COPELAND

An ex-Scottish cupboard-door wagon running in BR condition.
ROYE ENGLAND

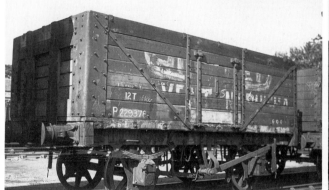

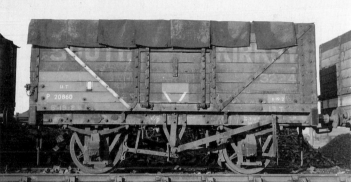

Left: *An ex-Staveley wagon with some original lettering visible; these wagons carried advertisements of the company's products, i.e. caustic soda, bleaching powder, etc. Note the self-contained buffers and Ellis axleboxes. We can see evidence of three liveries on these wagons with traces of the original pre-war lettering, the wartime small wording and the final BR 'P' numbering.* Right: *An ex-South Kirkby wagon with 'P' numbering on lighter colour patches, which probably obscured the wartime lettering. This picture was taken on 26th November 1951 when the livery was noted as grey with white lettering.*
ROYE ENGLAND

An ex-Scottish wagon from the Wemyss Coal Co., Fife, photographed at Coventry on 30th April 1955. It appears to have been a 1923 RCH design but note the 'D' dropper end-door catches, also the 4-plank side door. This wagon, with its various unpainted planks, shows a typical condition of a wagon in later life.
H. F. WHEELLER

*This shows the typical
state of wagons at the
end of their lives,
unpainted woodwork
and only a patch to
provide a background
for numbers.*
P. J. GARLAND
WESSEX
COLLECTION
A. ATTEWELL
ROGER SPELLER

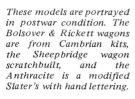

These models are portrayed in postwar condition. The Bolsover & Rickett wagons are from Cambrian kits, the Sheepbridge wagon scratchbuilt, and the Anthracite is a modified Slater's with hand lettering.

This Monkton wagon has seen better days. It is a scratchbuilt model with POWsides lettering.

FINISHING OFF

BUFFERS

When all the painting and weathering is finished, the buffers and couplings can be fitted. I have used MJT buffer heads for all these wagons. Some wagons were fitted with coil springs and some with Exactoscale leaf springing. Whichever method is used, the buffer stocks and spring retainers are the same. These were described in the section dealing with Cambrian kits.

First, using a 1mm drill, I clean out the buffer stock to remove any paint, etc, and try the head to ensure it moves easily. If using coil springs, try these with the buffer head; I try to get the softest springing possible. The springs do vary and may need stretching or shortening to get this right. When all is well, the heads are retained with a little slice of cable sleeving slipped over the shank and secured with a spot of superglue. I find this an easier method than bending the shank over, and it is easier to get the buffers the same length.

The Exactoscale system uses a leaf spring across the back of the buffers similar to the real thing. Exactoscale also supply buffers which have separate heads and shanks, and are assembled with Loctite. I had already drilled the buffer stocks to accept MJT heads, so I stuck with them, but the method of assembly is exactly the same.

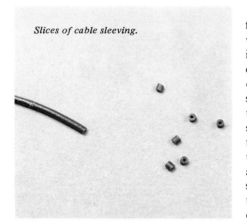

Slices of cable sleeving.

The buffer heads are fitted exactly as for the coil springs and the length adjusted with the piece of cable sleeving. The hole in the centre of the spring must be an easy fit over the hook shank. This system depends on having the shank of the hook sticking through the headstock to locate the spring and allow the neoprene sleeving to be slid on to retain it. I found the spring needs a little tweaking to get the buffers working satisfactorily. When all is OK, a washer is fitted between the spring and buffer shank. It is also possible to have a sprung drawhook using these components.

Buffer heads assembled with internal coil springs and retained with tiny slices of cable sleeving.

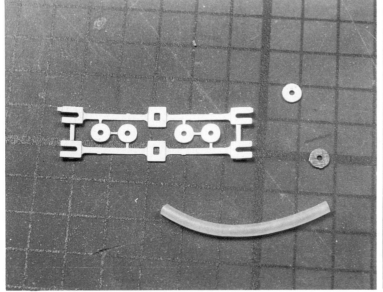

Left: *The component parts of Exactoscale leaf springing.* Right: *The spring assembled, the washers fit between the spring and the slice of cable sleeving.*

THREE-LINK COUPLINGS

Bending up the links is made very easy with a simple tool made from some 1mm x 3.5mm brass strip (Flack). The edges were rounded off for about an inch on both sides and a 0.5mm hole drilled close to the end. I fitted a handle to mine, which makes it more comfortable in use. The business end is bent at about 20°. This is to allow the handle to be out of the way when cutting the links which are made from 0.45mm brass or nickel silver wire. The end of a length of wire is pushed through the 0.5mm hole and using pliers, wound tightly for about a dozen turns round the jig. The links are cut off with a very fine piercing saw while holding them in a smooth-jawed vice.

Before fitting to the wagons, these were chemically blackened.

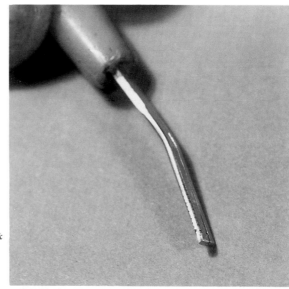

Tool for making 3-link coupling links.

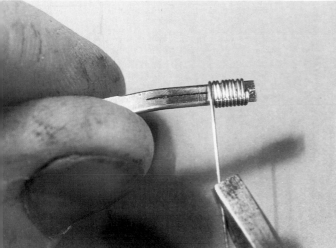

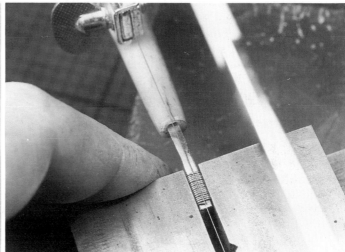

Left: *This shows the tool in use. The wire is pushed through the hole and wound as tightly as possible.* Right: *Cutting the links — holding them in a vice like this, they stay in one place. The bend in the jig allows the saw to miss the handle.*

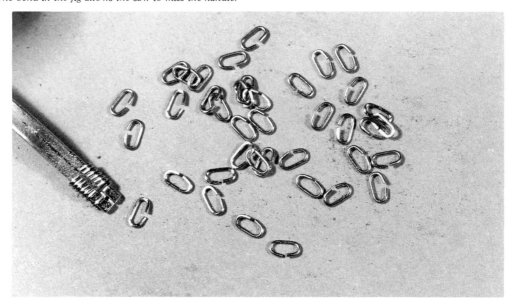

Here is the result of a few minutes work.

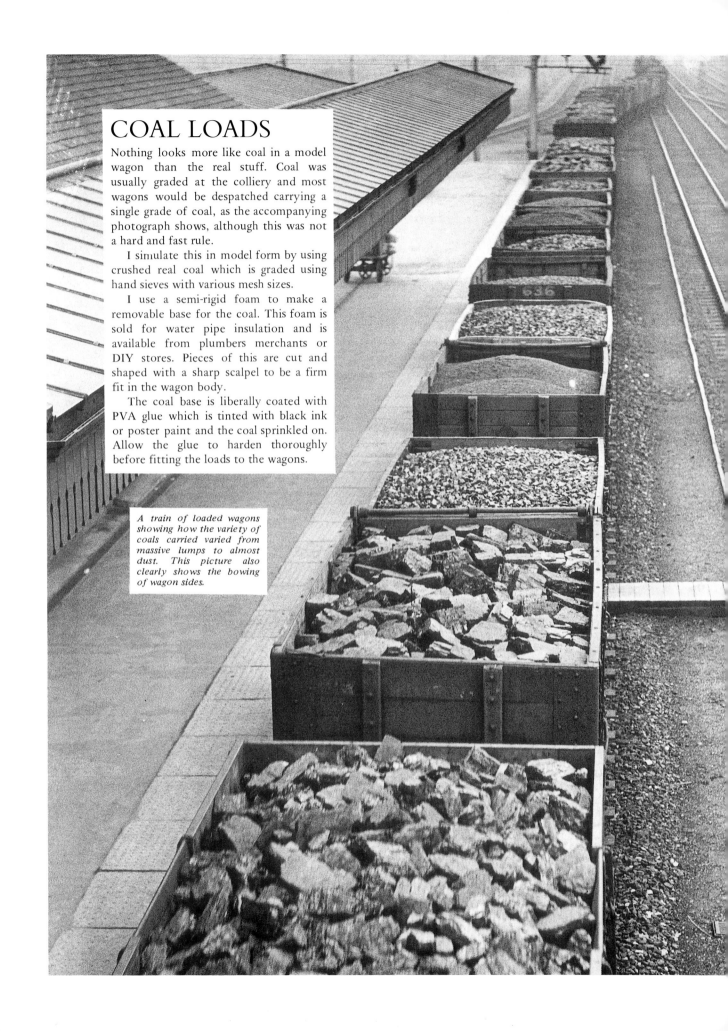

COAL LOADS

Nothing looks more like coal in a model wagon than the real stuff. Coal was usually graded at the colliery and most wagons would be despatched carrying a single grade of coal, as the accompanying photograph shows, although this was not a hard and fast rule.

I simulate this in model form by using crushed real coal which is graded using hand sieves with various mesh sizes.

I use a semi-rigid foam to make a removable base for the coal. This foam is sold for water pipe insulation and is available from plumbers merchants or DIY stores. Pieces of this are cut and shaped with a sharp scalpel to be a firm fit in the wagon body.

The coal base is liberally coated with PVA glue which is tinted with black ink or poster paint and the coal sprinkled on. Allow the glue to harden thoroughly before fitting the loads to the wagons.

A train of loaded wagons showing how the variety of coals carried varied from massive lumps to almost dust. This picture also clearly shows the bowing of wagon sides.

Here is the pipe lagging foam I used to make the coal base . . . and one cut ready to fit.

Applying a good layer of PVA.

A load of ungraded coal, possibly for locomotive use. This photo was taken at Lydney Jcn on 30th June 1951, the photographer noting the livery as lake or weathered red oxide with white lettering shaded black.
ROYE ENGLAND

A coaling session in progress. Note the different grades. The coal is liberally spread over the glue and left to dry.

A Monkton wagon being unloaded in the early 1950s. The practice of propping side doors whilst unloading was against the rules.
ROYE ENGLAND

The model will make a nice set piece at the end of a coal siding.

WEIGHTING OF MODELS

It is not easy to be specific about how much weight to put in model wagons, a lot will depend on the length of trains likely to be run and quality of trackwork. Clearly, for short trains with only a few wagons, weight is not too critical whereas with longer trains weight must be kept to the minimum.

I have found that about 50g per vehicle is adequate for compensated and sprung stock if one's trackwork is well laid; it is really a question of trial and error. What is more important is to keep the weight of stock consistent as a train of vehicles of different weights can cause problems, especially when being propelled.

The material I use for weights is ordinary lead flashing. This is approximately 1/16in thick by 6in wide and is available from builders merchants, who can usually supply small quantities. It is easily cut with scissors and fitted with epoxy to the underside of wagons (see photo of the slope-sided mineral wagon on page 42). If the model is to be loaded, it is easier to fit the weight inside the wagon.

SUPPLIERS OF PARTS AND MATERIALS

Eileen's Emporium (Roger Sawyer), P.O. Box 14753, London SE19 2ZH.
Tools and materials, wire, sheet, etc.

John Flack, 1 Meadow Bank, Kilmington, Nr. Axminster, Devon.
Brass and nickel wire and sheet. Also supplies Evergreen styrene materials.

Fourtrack Models (1992), 22 Grange Road, Harrow Middlesex, HA1 2PP.
Supplier of wagon kits, materials including Evergreen products and Zap-a-gap glues. Good mail order.

Ambis Engineering Division, 27 Stanhope Gardens, Ilford, Essex, IG1 3LQ.
Etched wagon underframe components.

Masokits Masterbits, 27 Crotch Crescent, New Marston, Oxford, OX3 0JL.
Etched wagon brake gears, sprung W-irons, etc.

ABS Models, 36 Field Barn Drive, Weymouth, Dorset, DT4 0ED.
Suppliers of whitemetal wagon kits and accessories.

Slater's Plastikard Ltd., Temple Road, Matlock Bath, Matlock, Derbyshire, DE4 3PG.
PO wagon kits, Plastikard sheet and strip, Mek-pak solvent.

R. D. Whyborn, 19 Glent Avenue, Headless Cross, Redditch, B97 5HH. (Exhibitions and mail order only)
Supplies own range of pre-printed wagons.

Exactoscale Ltd., 29 Couchmore Avenue, Esher, Surrey, KT10 9AS.
Etched brake gear, buffer springing and springing units for rolling stock.

D & S Models, 46 The Street, Wallington, Nr. Baldock, Herts, SG7 6SW.
Cast wagon kits, etched W-irons and wagon fittings.

Ultrascale Wheels, Gear Services Letchworth, The Wynd East, Letchworth, Herts, SG6 3EL.

Woodhead Models (Nigel Annand), 1 Evans Grove, St. Albans, Herts, AL4 9PJ.
Wagon lettering.

POWsides, Poplars Farm, Aythorpe Roding, Dunmow, Essex, CM6 1RY.
PO wagon sides in dry print lettering plus pre-printed kits.

Fox Transfers/Cranberry Graphics, Mail order service, 138 Main Street, Markfield, Leics, LE67 9UX.
Waterslide transfers BR freight stock.

Cambrian Models, 1 Sand Street, Milverton, Taunton, Somerset, TA4 1JN.
PO wagon kits.

Alan Gibson (workshop), The Bungalow, Church Road, Lingwood, Norwich, NR13 4TR.
Etched underframes, strapping plus cast buffers, etc.

Nathan Shestopal, Unit 2, Sapcote Trading Estate, 374 High Road, Willesden, London NW10 2DH.
General tool supplies, Vallorbe files.

Cooper Tools, Sealing Road, Wear 6, Washington, Tyne and Wear, NE38 9B7.
Weller soldering irons.

Carr's solders and fluxes, available from exhibitions or Home of O Gauge, 528 Kingston Road, Raynes Park, London SW20 8DT.

MJT Scale Components, 41 Oak Avenue, Shirley, Croydon, CR0 8EP.
Etched W-irons, cast wagon fittings.

Dragon Models, 9 Kingsley Close, Sully, Vale of Glamorgan, CF64 5UW.
Rub-down transfers for Welsh PO wagons and pre-group railways.

Phoenix Precision Paints Co., PO Box 359, Cheltenham, Glos. GL52 3YN.

D. J. Hornsby, 25 Manwood Avenue, Canterbury, Kent, CT2 7AH.
Large range of brass and plated pins.

FURTHER READING

British Goods Wagons. R J. Essery, D. P. Rowland & W. O. Steel (David & Charles).
Coal Trade Wagons. L. Tavender.
Railway Equipment Drawings. L. Tavender.
Private Owner Wagons Vols 1-3. Bill Hudson (OPC).
Private Owner Wagons Vol 4, Bill Hudson (Headstock).
Private Owner Wagons. Bill Hudson (Oakwood Press).
Private Owner Wagons. Peter Mathews (MAP).
Modellers Sketchbooks of Private Owner Wagons. A. G. Thomas (Model Railway Manufacturing Co. Ltd.).
LNER Wagons. Peter Tatlow (OPC).
LMS Wagons Vol. 1. R. J. Essery (OPC).
The LMS Wagon. Essery and Morgan (David & Charles).
Official drawings of LMS Wagons, Vols 1 & 2. R. J. Essery (Wild Swan Publications).
'Scratchbuilding model wagons'. Chris Crofts. *Model Railway Journal Nos. 12, 13, 14, 15.*
The 4mm Wagon Vol. 1. Geoff Kent (Wild Swan Publications).
'The 16-ton steel mineral wagon, prewar to BR'. Peter Fidczuk. *Modellers Back Track Vol. 1, Nos. 3, 4, 5.*
British Railways Wagons. Don Rowland (David & Charles).
B.R. Wagons Vol. 1. Bartlett et al (OPC).
B.R. Wagons, opens and hoppers. G. Gamble (Cheona Publications).
Pre-Nationalization Freight Wagons on B.R. Larkin (Bradford Barton).
'Modelling steel mineral wagons from kits'. Peter Tatlow. *Model Railway Journal Nos. 54, 55, 56, 57, 71, 77, 86 and 107.*
The Art of Weathering. Martyn Welch (Wild Swan Publications).
Private Owner Wagons on the Cambrian by Mike Lloyd (Welsh Railways Research Circle).
Private Owner Wagons of the Ince Waggon and Ironworks Co. A. J. Watts (HMRS).